QUEEN

THESE
ARE
THE
DAYS
OF
OUR
LIVES

QUEEN

THESE ARE THE DAYS

OF OUR LIVES

by Stephen Rider

Kingsfleet Publications
The Power House, Tandridge Court Farm, Tandridge Lane, Oxted, Surrey RH8 9NJ

CONTENTS

ACKNOWLEDGEMENTS

Phil, Chris, $teve, Tony S, Geoff, Alan,
Mum and Dad (good luck with yours
Dad!), Caroline, Peter, Ros, Tony, Andy T,
Joe, Mark, Jax, Jo, Penni, Sam, and Dave.

TO ALL THE PEOPLE WHO STOOD IN
MY WAY: ??*!!"$**!!!

INTRODUCTION

Album sales in excess of eighty million, twenty U.K. Top Ten singles, sixteen Top Ten albums, four albums in the U.K. Top Twenty at the same time, fifty naked girls on bicycles...

The list of Queen's achievements goes on forever, a staggering display of statistics that no other band has even managed to equal. Incredible. But statistics they are, mere numbers in a book that will impress hundreds of future generations, but which cannot give insight into the personalities behind such achievements, or the musical rainbow they created.

It is more impressive perhaps that a sixteen-year-old boy called Brian May carved his own guitar out of a mahogany fireplace, and that that guitar, like Sparky's piano, has remained his closest companion for twenty years. Or that an insecure young Persian immigrant dedicated his life to becoming the most outrageous character in rock'n'roll history, suffering bigotry, criticism and his own sexuality in the process - and literally died for his art. There will never be an artist more obsessed with entertaining people than Freddie Mercury.

It is that kind of love and dedication that nurtured and tortured Queen into shape in the first place. With the wild rock'n'roll abandon of Roger Taylor adding a hard-edged appeal to the band, and John Deacon's stoic, unswerving backbone, Queen were the complete band. Four very individual characters bouncing off each other's egos like a well-synchronised ping-pong match.

In March 1974, this strange hotch-potch of alteregos arrived. Stunning the TV nation on Top Of The Pops with their revolutionary second single, `Seven Seas Of Rhye', the legend was born. But, of course, Queen's story begins much further back than that, a long long way away, on an island called Zanzibar...

CHAPTER ONE

NOW I'M HERE
1946-1959

*"I was a very insecure young boy, probably
because I was a bit sheltered."*
(Freddie Mercury)

Zanzibar lies twenty-two-and-a-half miles off
the coast of East Africa. The island has
belonged to the British Commonwealth
since 1890, but in December 1963, it gained
independence within the Commonwealth, and in
1964 merged with Tanganyika, on the mainland.
Zanzibar and Tanganyika are now jointly known
as Tanzania. The city of Zanzibar itself was a
leading port in the export of cloves, coconuts and
soap.

When Frederick Bulsara was born on the island
on 5th September 1946, his father Bomi was
working as an accountant for the British
Government at the Beit El Ajaib, the `House Of
Wonders', built by the Sultan Barghash in the late
nineteenth century. Bomi and his wife Jer were of
Persian extraction, strict adherers to the Parsee
faith, descended from the Zoroastrians who
emigrated from Persia to India in the eighth
century.

Because of his parents' unerring dedication to
their faith, and his father's demanding job,

Freddie's upbringing was strict and spiritually solemn. His father was a foreboding figure revered by the young boy, but the two had little time to get to know each other, such were the demands of Bomi's diplomatic position. The rare occasions Freddie was allowed to visit him at his place of work were treated with great pomp and circumstance.

But his early years weren't totally devoid of sunshine. Often, the slightly awkward, bucktoothed boy would be seen diving in and out of stalls at local bazaars, enjoying the hubbub and clatter of Arab traders selling their wares, listening in fascination to the incessant sales patter. The child may have been lonely, having only a sister, Kashmira, six years his junior for company, but he made friends with the local traders. And he would spend many hours staring, in quiet reverence, at the breath-taking architecture and spiritual beauty of the mosques that rose in almost obscene majesty from the dusty, stone-cobbled streets. These were scenes and images that Freddie would never forget. Colour and flamboyance were already impressing themselves on the young boy.

When Freddie was still only a small boy, the family decided to ring the changes. Bomi had been offered a job in Bombay, and decided it was too good a prospect to turn down. Taking Freddie with him, he set off for Bombay, whilst Jer returned to England with Kashmira to set up home. Bomi and Freddie would follow in due course.

As soon as father and son arrived in Bombay, Freddie was sent off to boarding school (St Peter's Boarding School). Once again, he was denied the chance to get close to his father - indeed he'd been isolated from his entire family virtually overnight. He was beginning to resent the lack of attention, especially as a lively and creative mind was developing behind those dark eyes. But it was to be a long time yet before Freddie would be allowed to exercise his imagination. First he had to learn the art of survival, courtesy of his boarding school:

"You had to do what you were told, so the sensible thing was to make the most of it. I didn't particularly like being told what to do all the time, but I can see it did me a lot of good. I learnt to look after myself, and I grew up very quickly."

By the time he and his father moved to England in 1959, when Freddie was thirteen, the teenager felt fit to take on the world. But it was to be a short-lived burst of confidence.

The culture-shock took Freddie a long time to get over. The pokey, grey-skied claustrophobia of England was worlds away from the raw beauty of Zanzibar and India. And the people were so different: pale, clipped, judgmental strangers living in their tidy, uncluttered environments, seemingly oblivious to the world beyond their back gardens.

To thirteen-year-old Freddie, so ethnically different to most people he met, it was a frightening reality. At school, he was an outsider struggling with a strange new language. His colour and accent were the subject of much ridicule and, at first, Freddie was forced to withdraw into his shell.

That sense of insecurity and alienation was probably what turned Freddie into the attention-seeking animal we all knew and loved. Rather than bowing under the pressure of prejudice, he slowly but surely learnt that the only way to survive was to become a parody of himself. If people were going to take the piss out of his buck teeth, he would just have to bite back, show them he didn't care...

Freddie grew into his role of extrovert, and played it to extremes, just to make sure that nobody would forget him! But underneath the seemingly impervious exterior the sensitive soul still existed. Yet if people were growing to love the exterior so much, how could Freddie ever shed the flamboyance again? He had created an image from which he would never be able to escape.

Freddie's new home was in the Feltham district of Hounslow, Middlesex, a tiny, semi-detached Victorian house almost beneath the flight-path for Heathrow Airport. Just around the corner, in fact, from the home of a rather promising young scholar by the name of Brian May....

CHAPTER TWO

FATHER TO SON
1947-1964

"We had thought of music only as a hobby to Brian..."
(Harold May)

Brian Harold May was born to Harold and Ruth (née Fletcher) May on 19th July 1947, at Gloucester House Nursing Home, in the leafy London suburb of Hampton Hill, Twickenham, Middlesex. His home in Feltham was a semi-detached, thirties-style abode with all the usual middle-class comforts, including a black-and-ginger cat called Squeaky...

Brian had a comfortable, if unremarkable, childhood. An only child, he took to his school work like a duck to water, even at his first school, Hanworth Road Primary School in Feltham, where he first enrolled at the age of five. At eleven, he was showing sufficient promise to win a scholarship to Hampton Grammar School, where he was to become a star Physics student and eventually gain ten `O' levels and three `A's.

Although it was taken for granted that Brian's academic brilliance would lead to a career in Astro-physics, there was another talent lurking beneath the veneer. Young Brian was often heard singing along to his favourite songs on the radio ("even though I never knew what the words meant!"), particularly numbers by his heroine, Connie Francis. When he was as young as seven-years-old, his father organised piano lessons for him at a music school in Baker Street, where he studied up to fifth grade. He also bought Brian his first small acoustic guitar, and started teaching him George Formby numbers on the ukelele. The object at the time was merely to give Brian a worthwhile hobby. But I wonder if Harold May ever imagined that that hobby would develop into such an all-consuming passion?

Brian's parents may have been disappointed when their quiet, thoughtful son eventually opted for a musical career, as he undoubtedly would've become a respected astro-physicist in his alternative life. But his musical instincts were stronger than the academic and, as such, Harold and Ruth supported Brian's decision all the way, although it wasn't easy as Harold explained during Queen's early years:

"All through his childhood, music had been Brian's main hobby, but we had thought of it only as a hobby, even though we are a musical family."

In fact, it wasn't until the `Queen II' album was released in 1974 that the Mays would realise Brian's full musical potential. It's ironic then that, but for Harold's skill as an Electronics Engineer (working for the Ministry Of Defence) and Brian's own physics knowledge, his astonishing musical career might not have started at all...

Birth Of The `Red Special'

It was at the age of sixteen that Brian really started to get the rock'n'roll itch. He desperately wanted to start his own band, so that he could emulate the success of his own particular idols: Lonnie Donegan, Buddy Holly, The Yardbirds and The Stones. Unfortunately, the stratocaster on sale in the local guitar shop was way beyond his means and, for a while, Brian's dreams were shattered. But there was an alternative.

With their combined knowledge of electronics and physics, Brian and his father realised they could build their own guitar. In fact, it dawned on Brian that he could make a guitar better than any manufactured instrument, because it would be customised to his exact specifications. And, as father and son progressed with the guitar, they discovered that most existing instruments were riddled with fundamental design faults. Applying this knowledge to the new guitar, they managed to iron out most of the problems and build, in effect, a proto-type for a better design.

Converting the spare bedroom of the family house into a small workshop, father and son started their ambitious project to create the remarkable `Red Special', the guitar Brian would use throughout his career with Queen. It would take them two long years to perfect the instrument, Brian eagerly cycling home from school each day during his third and fourth years to help his father.

First they had to find a piece of wood to carve the body of the guitar from. The mahogany surround of their one-hundred-and-twenty year old fireplace would do nicely.

After carving the body and neck of the guitar into what would now be termed a Gibson `SG' shape, Brian and Harold built a steel truss rod into the neck. They'd noticed that on many existing electric guitars, the pressure on the strings would sometimes be so great (up to three-and-a-half hundredweight!) that it would bend the neck. The rod, held in place with a steel bolt, is still stoically doing its job almost thirty years later.

Brian then persuaded his Mum to surrender her mother-of-pearl buttons from her button-box to make the fretboard. Next, Brian and Harold designed an adjustable bridge to overcome the problem of snapping strings. Harold:

"We realised that with many guitars, when the strings are tightened over the bridge as the tremolo arm is used, it has a sawing effect that can wear the strings down. We designed a set of small rollers which don't put any wear and tear on the strings at all."

Another problem they discovered was that, in those days, when a tremolo arm was applied, it hardly ever returned to its original position, thus taking the guitar out of tune. The solution? Two motor-bike valve springs from a 1928 Panther bike to balance the arm. The arm itself was made out of a piece of stainless steel from the blade of a knife. (Since those days, guitar manufacturers have found their own solution to the tremolo arm problem: the tremolo block and bridge are built as one piece.)

Pick-ups were last on the list. Brian had noticed that on many guitars, the pick-ups were designed so that the guitarist couldn't get any feedback, as he recalls:

"Feedback was exactly what I wanted from the `Red Special', and nowadays any good guitarist thrives on it. Hendrix was the first to use feedback onstage. The thing is to let the strings feed back rather than the pick-ups. When you get the strings feeding back, you get the whole guitar singing, but using just the pick-ups results in a really awful whining sound."

Resourceful as ever, Brian made his own, using a little Meccano wheel which was built to wind around four thousand turns of wire on each of the three pick-ups. Harold:

"The secret of these pick-ups is in the position that each one is set because this alters the tonal harmonic effect, and by some really clever switching you can have any combination of twenty-four tones. When you listen to Brian's solo on `Brighton Rock' (off `Sheer Heart Attack'), you can hear him accompanying himself, using echoes.."

At a total cost of eight pounds, the Red Special was finished. Or was it? One thing was missing.... Ah, of course, a sixpenny piece! Just for good measure, and because Brian wasn't going to find a plectrum he liked for a long time yet, the sixpenny piece became his trademark.

With guitar in hand, Brian was now ready to start his first band, `1984'. The band, comprising Hampton Grammar pupils Tim Staffell on vocals, Dave Dilloway on rhythm guitar, John Garnham on bass, and local drummer Richard Thompson, formed in 1964. Spurred on by another school group called The Others who, by the time `1984' started, had already appeared on television (and released a single, `Oh Yeah'), Brian's band rehearsed hard. Using their lunch hours and evenings to practise at a school in

Whitton (next to Twickenham rugby ground), the band were regarded as `socially unacceptable' by their own rather short-sighted school authorities:

"It was daft. We weren't allowed to play at Hampton Grammar for some reason, coz rock music was unacceptable, not cultural. It was ridiculous, because rock was definitely becoming popular. We'd go and see bands around Richmond and Twickenham, and I saw people like The Yardbirds, The Stones and Clapton at a local club - they were really hot news!"

In fact, both Paul Samwell-Smith and Jim McCarty of The Yardbirds were `old boys' at Hampton Grammar, which was fast turning into a breeding ground for rock'n'roll hopefuls.

`1984' played their debut gig at St Mary's Church Hall, Twickenham, near Eel Pie Island - Brian's first-ever public performance. On that particular night, in 1964, the band were also joined by a keyboard-player, who'd built his own bizarre synthesiser: a harmonica attached to an electric hair-dryer and a small keyboard!

With primitive May-composed numbers like `Itsy-Bitsy Spider' and `Happy Hendrix Polka', and covers of Everly Brothers, Beatles and Hendrix numbers, the band, decked out in old military uniforms, soon made a name for themselves at regular dance hall and boating club gigs in the area. Brian, himself, was gaining a reputation for his rapid guitar runs. He was, in fact, on his way to becoming `really hot news' himself - at least in Twickenham!

Although `1984' split three years later, Brian and vocalist Tim Staffell stuck together when they both moved to London to further their respective academic careers in Astro-Physics and art. Tim would turn out to be a vital catalyst in the formation of Queen, as we will discover later.

As Brian took his first unsteady steps towards musical nirvana, eighteen-year-old Frederick Bulsara was rising above prejudice as a talented art student. He enrolled at Ealing College of Art, where he would later meet fellow art student Tim Staffell.

Meanwhile, down in Truro, Cornwall, a blonde blue-eyed boy called Roger Meddows Taylor was struggling to fulfil his love of music. Unfortunately, *his* parents, unlike Harold and Ruth May, were none too keen on Roger's ambitions. They wanted Roger to spend his life probing inside people's mouths...

CHAPTER THREE

DON'T STOP ME NOW
1949-1971

*"I've always been a fidget.
I can never sit still for long."*
(Roger Taylor)

Roger Meddows Taylor was born on 26th July 1949 to Michael and Winifred (née Hickman) Meddows Taylor at West Norfolk and Kings Lynn Hospital. Roger's first brush with music happened after he and his sister Clare moved to Truro, Cornwall, with their parents when he was just eight. Enrolling at Truro Cathedral School, it wasn't long before the angelic little boy proved himself a talented soprano in the choir, and he continued his high-pitched warbling for a year.

At this stage, of course, Roger hadn't formulated any ideas on a career, but it became evident that his parents already had their son's future mapped out. Little did they know that Roger would completely thwart their attempts to guide him in the `right direction'. Though he always looked as if butter wouldn't melt in his mouth, Roger was never quite as angelic as he looked!

At eleven, he transferred to Truro Public School as a dayboy. Roger hated the experience, but: "At least I wasn't a boarder. I'd hardly ever have seen home, and would have had no freedom at all. And I'd never have been able to play in a group."

As it was, in 1963, Roger took up the guitar, against his parents' wishes, before finally settling on drums. Playing with various school bands, including one called Reaction, he soon gained a solid reputation as a vocalist/drummer in the Truro area. His influences at the time?:

"When I was a really young kid, I was inspired by Elvis Presley, Jerry Lee Lewis, Little Richard, all the really early rockers. Because I didn't even have a record-player at the time, I had to keep going round my cousin's to listen to stuff on his `gramophone'. As I got older, my heroes changed a little: Jimi Hendrix, Bob Dylan, John Lennon, archetypal influences I suppose, but why not? They were the kind of musicians who made statements within their music, and I respected that."

The more Michael and Winifred tried to halt his progress as a musician, the more their son deliberately set out to forge a career as a serious skinbeater. As it turned out, Roger's parents won the first round.

Leaving Truro School in 1967 with a commendable seven O-levels and three A's (in Biology, Chemistry and Physics), Roger buckled under family pressure and agreed to take a course in Dentistry. He did, however, have ulterior motives for joining the Dental College in London (officially called the London Hospital Medical College in Whitechapel):

"It was just a way of getting to London and

gaining a means of support from the student grant. Being a student was cool then." Well, not *that* cool, as Roger was to discover.

Dissecting and examining corpses on a daily basis, Roger found himself growing more and more despondent with his unchosen career. He gritted his teeth for a while, but eventually quit the gruesome training, eventually swapping over to a biology course at the North London Polytechnic in 1968. But Roger had not forgotten his sole reason for travelling to London. Whilst still on his dental course, he attended as many gigs as possible at neighbouring colleges, forging contacts along the way. And he would scour the newspapers and college bulletin boards in the hope that he'd find a good drum position. One day, in 1967, he did.

`Wanted: Ginger Baker type drummer' said the advertisement on the Imperial College noticeboard. It sounded perfect.

It was twenty-year-old astro-physics student and guitarist Brian May who had pasted up the advert on the Imperial College noticeboard. He and old buddy Tim Staffell invited Roger to join their band, Smile.

None of the band knew at the time that Tim's strange college friend, Freddie Mercury, who would hang around at their gigs, was to be their future vocalist instead of Staffell himself. Freddie himself didn't know, although the experience of watching Smile perform was beginning to rub off on him. He started to quietly plot his own attack on the music business, unaware that this band, Smile, was to be his stepping-stone to stardom!

Meanwhile, the unknown fourth member of Queen, John Deacon, was oblivious to the fortunes of Freddie, Brian or Roger. He was in his own world, way up north in Leicester, efficiently pursuing his own musical and academic careers...

> *"He's very solid and no nonsense.*
> *He's always got his feet firmly on the ground."*
> *(Brian May on John Deacon)*

John Richard Deacon was born on 19th August 1951 at St Francis' Private Hospital, London Road, Leicester, the son of Arthur Henry and Lilian Mollie (née Perkins) Deacon.

John was, on the surface, an unassuming little boy. Keeping his feelings very much to himself, nobody really knew what was going on behind those mysterious grey-green eyes. To this day, he has remained the real enigma in Queen, but that is only because he is a man who hates to waste words on frivolous talk.

John began his academic life at Oadby Infants' School in 1956. No doubt, even at such a young age, he toddled into his first class with eyes wide open, surveying the situation with a cool business approach, logistically working out his plan of attack!

As such, John was never regarded as a dynamic personality, because he simply got on with his work without any fuss, which is exactly what he went on to do as Queen's bass-player.

From Oadby Infants, John transferred to Gartree High School and, at the age of eleven, enrolled at Beauchamp Grammar School in Leicester where he would go on to achieve eight 'O' levels and three 'A's.

At eighteen, with his qualifications intact, John moved to London to pursue a degree course in Electronics at Chelsea College, part of London University. He would eventually earn himself a First Class Honours BSc degree.

However dedicated John was to his studies, he always maintained a keen interest in music from an early age. In 1965, at fourteen, he was already well-ensconced in local Leicester band, Opposition, and played his first-ever gig with them at Enderby Youth Club that year. Although when he first moved to London, he left his bass and equipment at his mother's home in Oadby (his father died when he was younger), it wasn't long before he decided to have his gear sent down, and he started performing in various small London outfits.

It was at one particular gig John played at a Chelsea disco in 1970 that Roger Taylor, Brian May and Freddie `Mercury' Bulsara (who had just joined Smile, and changed their name to Queen) spotted the talented bassist. Nothing happened at that point, but when John turned up for an audition with Queen in February 1971, the band remembered him. It had taken them six months to find the right man, but at last they'd found him. He was quiet and studious, hardly said a word throughout the audition, but John Deacon was also the most dynamic bass-player they'd ever seen.

Queen was complete. But the story wasn't.

CHAPTER FOUR

BACK CHAT
1959-1968

The missing links and the invaluable Staffell

When John Deacon passed the audition as Queen's bass-player, the band were officially born. But there are many gaps in the story. How did Freddie develop into such a colourful but mysterious personality between his arrival in England and enrolment at Ealing College Of Art? How did he become a vocalist? What about Brian's band `1984', and his budding astro-physics career? Read on...

Freddie's development from `Bulsara' to `Mercury' - that colourful, outrageous personality - was his way of shedding the immigrant conscience. When he moved with his parents to England, he was still at the relatively impressionable age of thirteen, still able to develop new characteristics and take in new surroundings. He knew he had to integrate into British society to survive, or spend the rest of his life a stranger in a strange country, as his parents seemed to be doing.

For Bomi and Jer Bulsara, initiating themselves into a new culture was not even a consideration. They were not about to sacrifice a lifetime's customs and beliefs just to get on with a society they were forced to live in. They retreated into their beloved Parsee shells and refused to take any part in British society. Bomi's new job in the Accounts Department at Forte's was somewhat of a come-down from the exotic diplomatic positions he'd held in Zanzibar and India, so lack of self-respect must've contributed to their attitudes.

When their son began to reject the background and culture they held so sacred, it must've appalled them. But how else could Freddie have survived, made friends, in this foreign country? He had to become as British as those around him, or alienate himself from this new society.

Sadly, the more he grew into his environment, the more he grew apart from his parents. He could no longer root himself to a doctrine that had no relevance to his new life.

Still, it's obvious that, subconsciously at least, Freddie always maintained a little of the Parsee. The wild splashes of colour that made up so much of his personality were surely borne from the vivid hues of Zanzibar and India the arrogant poise a throwback to his Persian ancestry... Freddie never forgot the visual beauty of his childhood environment. Creatively, he had a lifetime's material from his memories of yesteryear.

He was, in any case, highly imaginative from an early age, and that imagination manifested itself first into artistic talent, and later into music. And it was always apparent in his demeanour and in the way he dressed. Freddie oozed imagination, flaunted colour.

As his parents withdrew more and more into their bubble of Zoroastrianism, Freddie positively threw off its shackles of conformity. By attempting to ignore it completely, never speaking of his background to anyone, his reputation for being an `enigma' developed.

At school, he wasn't particularly bright, showing a penchant for the more creative subjects, rather than the academic. He took piano lessons, passing each exam easily, and eventually reaching Grade Five. As such, his enrolment at art college for an Art and Design Diploma course, around 1964, was predictable, and it was here that Freddie really began to turn into a decadent `arty-type' character, changing his name from Bulsara to `Mercury', after the Greek mythological god. As Freddie commented once:

"Art School teaches you to be more fashion-conscious, to be always one step ahead."

At Ealing Art College (a hive of musical activity, spawning the likes of Pete Townshend and Ron Wood), he met Tim Staffell of deceased Middlesex outfit `1984' (purely by coincidence), so Tim's memories of Freddie retreat further back than any of Queen's. He would frequently visit the Bulsara home in Feltham during college holidays, and it was he who noticed how conscious Freddie's family were of their ancestry. Tim remembers how much his good friend changed during those early years, and it's obvious that Staffell's influence and contacts had an affect on Freddie.:

"Freddie was very different when I first knew him. When Jimi Hendrix first started, Freddie absolutely idolised him. He was his god. At college, he used to spend a lot of his time drawing pictures of Jimi, and I can remember him miming in the art room, holding a twelve-inch ruler like a microphone, throwing back his head as he mimed the songs (a poise that would become his trademark). Hendrix was everything to him, and I suspected that it ran a great deal deeper than just the music.

"Hendrix was a negro from the ghetto who'd pulled himself up by his boot-straps and become totally accepted by everyone, black and white, because of the quality of his music. Although Freddie wasn't impoverished and living in a ghetto, I think Hendrix represented something to him, a goal that he could achieve himself.

"At that time, when I first knew him at college, the idea of being a star as such, or even a singer, hadn't formulated yet. He knew he wanted to do something special, but didn't have a direction yet. So it was fascinating to watch him as the years went on, forming his plan of attack!

"I remember him in the early days at college wearing dark grey jackets, it may have been a suit even, with those old-fashioned Bri-nylon shirts with the tiny collars, and a thin little tie. When we started going round together, he'd come with me when I went off to play gigs with Smile, and he'd stand there at the back or at the side of the stage listening to us play. Even though he never came up onstage at all, I could see he was starting to get interested in the music."

Through Tim, Freddie met drummer Roger Taylor, with whom he would set up a Kensington Market stall. And he met Brian, Smile's guitarist who had been his unknown neighbour for so many years....

From 1964 to 1967, `1984' gigged constantly around the Twickenham area (even after Brian had left school and gone on to his degree course), gaining respect as one of the most promising bands in the locality. Indeed, they even won a talent contest at the Top Rank in Croydon, winning a reel of tape and a CBS album of their choice (they picked Simon & Garfunkel). And Brian was developing as a proficient singer as well as guitarist, much to the envy of Staffell, the band's own lead vocalist:

"Occasionally, we'd play a few ballads. Brian used to sing `Yesterday' which used to get screams and applause, and made me dead jealous!"

Perhaps the band would've gone on to greater heights if they hadn't scattered to their respective colleges. When Brian left for Imperial College, a year ahead of Tim Staffell, the difficulties began and, after each member had taken his turn to leave school, `1984' finally disintegrated in 1967.

But, in any case, Brian was wary of the music business, and that caution may've destroyed the band anyway. Even when Queen started to become a serious entity, he insisted on keeping one finger in the academic `pie'. Contracts, businessmen, accountants - these were all aspects that Brian feared would blemish the music itself. He just wanted to play. Thoughts of making money through music were as alien to him as England was to the Bulsaras. Ironic then that he would go on to become one of the highest-paid company directors in the country!

So `1984' was purely a recreational group to Brian, although his time with them was, of course, valuable experience. His confidence grew the more people assured him of his rare talent for playing guitar. But he was also intent on becoming an `all round' musician, continuing to play his dad's ukelele (complete with beer stains from Harold May's days in the war), as well as learning techniques on the Jew's harp (which can be heard on `A Day At The Opera'), tin whistle (!) and mouth organ. And he was also starting to experiment with different sounds on the guitar itself, making it sound like many instruments. On `Good Company', off `A Night At The Opera', the result of these experiments can be heard in abundance, Brian making the Red Special sound like a trombone, a cello and a piccolo. For him, that kind of achievement was not just musically satisfying, but scientifically-so as well, because it meant that all the work he and his father had put into the guitar was paying off.

Whilst progressing in leaps and bounds musically, Brian was also continuing in his bid to become an Infra-Red Astronomer. It was still his intention to become a serious scientist and he threw himself into his `O' and `A' level studies in pursuance of a degree course.

Leaving Hampton Grammar with his ten `O's and three `A's, eighteen-year-old Brian strode purposefully into the Imperial College, Kensington. Three years later, he would fulfil his and his parents ambitions by achieving an Honours Degree in Physics and Maths. During those years, he also started training himself to be Infra-Red Astronomer and, in 1968, on the basis of his research, Professor Sir Bernard Lovell invited Brian to work at the Jodrell Bank Laboratory, whilst preparing his thesis to become a Doctor of philosophy. Brians father explained a few years later:

"Brian was preparing a thesis on zodiacal light, which are great showers of particles that can be seen at sunset and sunrise and which have never been satisfactorily explained. Before Queen started to become successful, he was doing private tutorials at Imperial College. He'd also constructed, to his own designs, special apparatus for the study of zodiacal light. The equipment had been shipped out to Tenerife in the Canary Islands so that observations could be recorded."

Brian would continue to work on his thesis right up until the recording of `Queen II', when he'd put his research aside in favour of his burnishing musical career. In any case, he was really never that convinced that he wanted to spend his entire life peering through telescopes:

"Astronomy's much more fun when you're not an Astronomer. Most of the time while I was studying was spent either making equipment, setting it up or else typing away at computers trying to analyse the results. The amount of time you actually spend looking at the stars is minimal. But now, in my spare time, I love to peer through telescopes, because it's just a hobby."

Brian would also decline Professor Lovell's offer because, by that time, 1968, his new band Smile would be making a fair amount of headway on the college circuit. Brian was beginning to show serious intent towards a musical career, over and above any scientific aspirations.

Smile had formed in 1967 immediately after the decline of `1984'. By then, Brian had been at Imperial for two years, Tim Staffell at Ealing Art College for a year. They were still the best of friends, and hadn't thought twice about forming another band together. A three-piece would be sufficient, so all they needed was a `Ginger Baker type drummer'. Enter Roger Taylor.

CHAPTER FIVE

PLAY THE GAME
1967-1969

Learning the hard way

S mile, at first, was merely an extension of `1984', with Brian and Tim incorporating more and more of their own material. As the band was only a trio, Staffell started to double up as both vocalist and bass-player:

"I can't clearly remember how or why it happened that I became a bassist! I bought a cheap Vox copy of a Fender Precision for thirty pounds, second hand, and then spent the first day sawing the tail-piece down so that it looked like a real Fender!"

Throughout their respective studies, Brian, Tim and Roger gigged hard with Smile, taking their repertoire predominantly round neighbouring colleges. Thus their rapidly-swelling fan base was built around a student hard-core. Smile were fast becoming known as `The Imperial College band'.

To take some responsibility off their shoulders, Smile started to get bookings through the Rondo Agency in Kensington High Street. The agency was in the same building as a mobile disco company called `Juliana's Discotheques', for whom Tim did some graphics work.

With a diary full of dates, it soon became apparent that the band would need some muscle to hump gear. Pete Edmunds, yet another ex-Hampton Grammar pupil, came in to drive their tiny green Ford Thames Van and act as roadie (he would later go on to work for Paul McCartney and Wings).

As well as playing round the London college circuit, Smile would occasionally nip down to Truro, Cornwall for the odd gig. These `mini tours' were arranged by Roger, and sometimes would only amount to one gig! But each trip was a welcome break for the boys who, by now, knew the inside of each London college like the backs of their hands. Tim:

"Those weekends in Cornwall were highlights of our time with Smile because everyone used to make such a fuss of us down there. It always became a great social thing with lots of drinking sessions. It was all so much more relaxed down there than in London, and everyone was so kind, inviting us into their homes and to parties and so on. Sometimes we'd crash on people's floors (including Pat and Sue Johnstone's, who would go on to run the Queen Fan Club), but if we were really lucky, we'd actually get beds to sleep in, and Roger's mother would put us up at her house, which was right in the centre of Truro.

"Occasionally, we'd make a stay of it and play at other venues apart from PJs, where we always played. Places like the Flamingo Ballroom in Redruth."

Of course, the band were always short of money in those days, being on student grants and earning only small rewards for their gigs (average fifteen pounds a night, although occasionally they'd make thirty pounds for a gig, which was hugely extravagant in those days!). It was obvious they weren't playing for the money. On one particular trip down to Cornwall, they were expecting twenty-five quid between them for the one gig. As it turned out, they didn't even get that! Tim:

"I remember we got as far as Andover when the engine seized up. We didn't know whether to blow out the gig or not. But then we phoned one of those firms that provides vans and drivers for musicians and their equipment, and they sent down a van and a bloke who drove us down to Truro for twenty-five quid, which meant that all our money'd gone before we'd even started to play! Not only that, but the bloke just dropped us off, turned round and drove straight back to London! So we were stranded in Truro with all our equipment.

"In the end, Brian and I caught the Cornish Riviera express back to London with all our guitars, drums and equipment in the guard's van. When we got back to Paddington, we walked straight through the barrier with all the gear on a trolley without anyone asking us to pay any extra. Richard Thompson, who'd been our drummer in 1984, picked us up at the station."

Funnily enough, in 1969, Richard was to play with Freddie Mercury in a band called Wreckage, thus knitting the circle even closer.

Meanwhile, in the same year, Smile were beginning to get noticed..

It was after a particularly good gig at The Speakeasy in 1969 that American producer Lou Reizner made himself known to the band backstage. He was Smile's first contact with a `real music business person', and perhaps they were a little overawed by the attention he was giving them. Reizner's offer sounded too good to be true to the green-gilled band. He was the man responsible for running the U.K. branch of the U.S. record company, Mercury, and he was offering Smile the chance to record their own single. What the band didn't realise was that Mercury had no actual base in Britain apart from a distribution arrangement, so it was hardly likely that a single would receive much airplay or attention here. Not only that, but they were only being offered a one-single deal, with no option for further recordings.

Smile eagerly signed the contract, and virtually sprinted into the studio to record what they hoped would be the single to catapult them to the stars.

As it turned out, the producer who worked with Smile would end up playing an important part in signing Queen to their first deal, so the experience wasn't without its far-reaching advantages. John Anthony produced Smile in Trident Studios where they recorded two songs, `Earth' (by Tim Staffell) and `Step On Me' (by May and Staffell).

The single failed to sell in the States, which doomed any chances of a release in the U.K. Tim Staffell, as major songwriter of the A and B sides, received a cheque for £1.10 in royalties, Brian and Roger making a fraction of that amount! Mercury, in fact, gave Smile one more chance, sending them into the new De Lane Lea Studios with producer Fritz Fryer to record four tracks. One of these was the May/Staffell-composed `Doing All Right', which was good enough to be included on Queen's first album four years later. Alas, none of the material was released at the time, although all the songs Smile recorded for Mercury appeared on a Japanese-only release in 1982.

Predictably, Smile were dropped from Mercury, and the disillusioned band returned to the college circuit, aware that they were now back at square one. Mercury's operations in the U.K. closed down shortly afterwards, Lou Reizner returning to the States for a while before coming back to Britain some years later to work on The Who's `Tommy' album.

Tim, Brian and Roger decided they could no longer depend on the band for financial support so, feet firmly back on earth, they each started looking for independent means of earning money. Brian took various part-time jobs in the summer recess: two weeks making windscreen wipers, and two months working at EMI Electronics assessing the destructive effects of fragmentation bombs. Although he found the latter interesting from a scientific point-of-view, he was none too happy about working on ways at maximising the killing effects of bombs.

Roger, meanwhile, decided to start a second-hand clothes stall at Kensington Market with Freddie Mercury, by now one of the band's closest friends. Roger remembers the eighteen months he and Freddie spent in Kensington Market:

"We used to sell lovely old velvet stuff with lace and also lots of old clothes which Freddie and I used to pick up going round rag merchants and junkyards. the biggest stroke of luck that we ever had was when we bought a hundred fur coats from a rag merchant in Battersea for fifty pence each - and then sold them all for between four and eight pounds. And that was still a bargain that we were offering. Then we had another good buy in forty Russian fox furs. When we bought those, we had our own full-length black velvet coats made up, and then trimmed each one with fox fur. And they looked beautiful when we were ready to sell them.

"We kept the stall on for about eighteen months, paying a rent of ten pounds a week. Those were good days with us making a good living and enjoying ourselves, because the market was run by musicians, actors, writers and artists; the sort of people who had ideas of their own, but who needed some little sideline like that to bring in some extra money. Then there'd always be people from different groups wandering around the market looking for clothes, and sometimes we'd serve film stars like Julie Christie. It was almost a life-style of its own with quite a few eccentrics. Now, that's all changed. Instead, it's run by the usual sort of people who run clothes and shoe shops and sell manufactured products."

Freddie, meanwhile, had left Ealing College Of Art with his Art And Design Diploma, and was becoming more and more extravagant in his dress and mannerisms. Still en route for a career that would allow his exhibitionist temperament free rein, he used Smile as his `study subject', tagging along with them wherever they went, and watching the band's every move. He had by now decided that music would be the vehicle to carry him to great heights and, as such, joined Liverpudlian band Ibex who, on arriving in London, had changed their name to

Wreckage (though they occasionally appeared as 'Sour Milk Sea' as well). Freddie became the band's vocalist and keyboard-player, with small contributions on guitar.

He became well-known on the local club/college circuit as an extremely arrogant, slightly camp performer who was, quite obviously, the focal point of Wreckage. In reality, without Freddie, Wreckage wouldn't have lasted five minutes, because he *was* the band. He would frequently be heard to shout impatiently to the other members in his band "We must have an *act!*", because the visual image was so important to him. People regarded Freddie as 'total Kensington Market': black velvet jackets and tight trousers, long black hair, silver jewellery and black nail varnish. He would tell people, with no qualms at all that "I am not going to become a star - I'm going to be a *legend!*". It wasn't a boast. For Freddie, it was just a fact of life. Already, he was beginning to behave like the star he would become. Freddie would never travel by public transport - he was above such things - and one day he even had the gall to sell Roger's jacket (accidentally left behind on the stall) to pay for a cab home! No doubt he got away with it too...

In retrospect, it was obvious Freddie always had his heart set on joining Roger and Brian in one capacity or another. He was massively ambitious, and saw Smile as the perfect vehicle for his own career. However, Tim Staffell was a good friend, and he was not about to usurp his position as Smile's vocalist. Wreckage would often appear on the same bill as Smile, and Freddie would use the opportunity to 'show' Brian and Roger what he could do, frequently offering them snippets of 'advice':

"Why are you wasting your time doing this? You should do more original material. You should be more demonstrative in the way you put the music across. If I was your singer, that's what I'd be doing!"

But he was not their singer - yet.

CHAPTER SIX

BREAKTHRU
1970-1971

"I am not going to be a star - I'm going to be a legend!" (Freddie Mercury)

Smile staggered on for a while but, after the Mercury Records incident, their hearts weren't really in the band anymore. It was a vicious circle. Brian, in particular, was now perhaps too wary of any involvement with the music business, so what could they do? Playing safe left them with no place to go, yet lunging at any more lucrative offers could be dangerous.

Smile did play one very impressive gig before the inevitable split happened. Supporting the likes of Free, Joe Cocker, The Bonzo Dog Doo Dah Band and Spooky Tooth, the band played a charity show at the Royal Albert Hall, which had been arranged by the Imperial College. Tim:

"I'll always remember that show because John Peel was introducing the bands, and when he announced our name, we all ran onstage enthusiastically... As I started to sing, I managed to pull out my mike lead, everything went dead and we had to start again! What an anticlimax! We started with our version of `If I Were A Carpenter', then continued with `Earth', `Mony Mony' and `See What A Fool I've Been' (which would appear on the B-side of the `Seven Seas Of Rhye' single in 1974), an old blues number that I first heard on a Sonny Terry and Brownie McGhee album.

"The hall wasn't packed that night, but it was still a great experience to go on stage and look out at an auditorium as large as that. It was the first time that any of us (notably Brian and Roger) had ever played anywhere like that."

Smile almost appeared at that gig as a four-piece. Discussions held beforehand were, perhaps, the band's last-ditch attempt to be positive about their future. The idea was to bring in a keyboard-player, and they even had a candidate, Chris, lined up for the show. Rehearsals prior to the day, however, proved unsuccessful and Brian, Tim and Roger blew him out the day before. They also tried out a pianist called Phil, who played temporarily with them, but that didn't work out either. It was the prelude to the end of Smile, as by now they'd started rowing heavily amongst themselves.

The final nail in Smile's coffin was Tim's decision to leave the band in the summer of 1970. He answered an ad in one of the music papers for a vocalist, and found himself singing for Humpy Bong, a moderately successful band of the era. The band, featuring ex-Bee Gee Colin Petersen, did at least appear on Top Of The Pops, but that was really their only claim to fame.

Brian and Roger were understandably depressed by this drastic turn of events, although the split - after three years - was inevitable. What were they supposed to do now?

The answer was just around the corner - in the hands of that outrageous exhibitionist Freddie Mercury. He, of course, had been waiting for the opportunity to link up with Brian and Roger - already planning their future together. In a sense, he'd been using both Smile and Wreckage to formulate his `grand attack' on the music business. Wreckage was Freddie's training ground, the school for him to practise his arrogant prancings, his cooings and poutings, to become the ultimate performer. Some may have resented his blasé attitude, but really it was Freddie's only way to assure success - to be single-minded, and to believe totally in his own talent.

Freddie used Smile as the example from which to learn by. Where Wreckage was the band he could practise on, Smile was the one he could learn from by watching their mistakes, and forming ideas to shape them into the ultimate band. The name would have to go of course... `Smile' was much too tame a name for him.

Without further ado, he boldly walked out on Wreckage, and virtually *told* Brian and Roger he was their new vocalist. At first, the two were reticent about Freddie's ideas for the band. Their brush with Mercury Records was still cutting deep, and Freddie's plans were all based on risk, all about sticking their necks out. What if it all backfired again?

Freddie was having nothing of their negative attitude. It was simple. First, their musical direction: to combine the heaviness of Led Zeppelin with a little pop. Second, the visual image: glamrock, complete with full-blown stage show. The overall picture? Something a little camp, and totally outrageous.

Brian and Roger nearly choked. The current musical fashion was heading towards heaviness, an overtly dark and masculine image, nothing glamorous at all in fact. What Freddie was suggesting was that they go totally against the grain. They could end up being the laughing-stock of the rock fraternity, and that would be it, the end of all their dreams.

On the other hand, if the plan *did* work, they'd have enough ammunition to hit three markets right between the eyes: hard rock, pop and the teenybopper market.

Then Freddie revealed the code-name for his operation. It was almost the final straw, and Brian and Roger's hysterical laughter could be heard all the way to Zanzibar... But Freddie was adamant:

"It's just a name, but it's very regal obviously, and it sounds splendid. It's a strong name, very universal and immediate. It had a lot of visual potential and was open to all sorts of interpretations. I was certainly aware of the gay connotations, but that was just one facet of it."

`Queen'. The name worried Brian and Roger to hell, but Freddie was taking them on such a rollercoaster of ideas, they hardly had time to argue.

For Freddie, life was certainly looking up, because not only had he found the perfect vehicle for his exhibitionist streak, but also an outlet for the romantic side of his character. Mary Austin, who worked on the managerial staff of Biba's, was everything Freddie needed, a stable, loving woman who did not regard his musical ideas and ambitions as either fantastical - or as competition. The two were inseparable and, not long after they met, they moved into a flat in Holland Park together. By now, Freddie's life was generally growing busier, as he was dividing his time between working at Kensington Market and doing the occasional graphic design jobs. He was on the books of a Chancery Lane agency, Austin Knights, who found him a freelance job illustrating for a childrens' space story. But he never finished the work, so busy was his life in other areas - and his mind, at present, was on finding a bass-player for Queen.

The band needed somebody who would complement the band, act as suitable rhythm partner for Roger and, at the same time, be prepared to take a backseat to Freddie who, by popular demand and natural right, was the focal point of Queen.

It was difficult. Whilst rehearsing, writing and playing only at friends' parties (as public gigs were out of the question without a bassist), the three tried out candidate after candidate, in vain, for six months. As it happened, the person they were looking for played in front of their very eyes at a Chelsea disco during that second half of 1970. But fate moves in mysterious ways, and the time was evidently not quite right yet.

So Queen ploughed through the bass-players, but none of them had the right personality or technique for them. There were two, in particular, who *appeared* to have the right chemistry. But Mike Grose lasted only one gig before they realised he wasn't what they were looking for. Barry Mitchell lasted a little longer, but only because Freddie, Brian and Roger needed someone to fill in till the right person turned up.

And, at last, he did. In February 1971, after

auditioning another string of hopefuls, twenty-year-old John Deacon walked into their lives. Brian remembers:

"We just knew he was the right one, even though he was so quiet. He hardly spoke to us at all."

And then there were four.

CHAPTER SEVEN

ONE VISION
1971-1972

*"The concept of Queen is to be regal and majestic.
Glamour is a part of us, and we want to be dandy..."*
(Freddie Mercury)

After much unintentional ducking and diving, Queen were assembled as one group. Four very individual characters... Freddie the bizarre exhibitionist with the enigmatic streak; Brian the ethereal minstrel with the looks of a medieval prince, but the logical, mathematical mind of the scientist he might've become; Roger, rock'n'roll animal with both gentle creativity and passion playing equal parts in his drumming style; and John, the bobbing bass-player with the cool business head, stoically holding the fort, occasionally permitting the barest of smiles to play across his lips....

"I was probably the one person in the group who could look at it from the outside, because I came in as the fourth person in the band. I knew there was something there, but I wasn't convinced of it...until possibly the `Sheer Heart Attack' album."

For John Deacon, Queen may not have appeared to be his means to an end. At first, he was as cynical as Brian and Roger but, like them, he found himself carried away on Freddie's pink-tinged cloud. But, like Brian and Roger, he continued with his studies, determined to keep at least some eggs out of the Queen basket! The combined cynicism is not to say they didn't believe Queen could make it. But Freddie's aspirations could just as well have been overblown pipe-dreams as realistic career moves. As it turned out, it would take three long years for the band to make serious headway. In the meantime, they wrangled long and hard over decisions to drop their respective careers. Brian:

"If we were going to drop the careers we'd trained hard for, we wanted to make a really good job of music. We all had quite a bit to lose, really, and it didn't come easy. To be honest, I don't think any of us realised it would take a full three years to get anywhere. It was certainly no fairytale."

Even Freddie held a certain amount of reserve:

"We said okay, we're going to take the plunge into rock and we're really going to do a job at it, no half measures. We all had potentially good careers and we weren't prepared to settle for second best if we were going to abandon all the qualifications we had got in other fields."

Whilst Brian continued with his thesis, John hurled himself into his last year of his Electronics course, which he would complete in July (with a First Class Honours Degree), and follow with a teaching job at a local comprehensive school in September - a job he kept right up to the success of the `Queen II' album in 1974. Roger and Freddie kept the market stall going. They were now selling not only second-hand clothes but artwork as well, earning sufficient money to keep Queen going.

Freddie was, indeed, using his artistic skills to the band's advantage. In typically arty fashion, he decided that Queen's logo should derive from each of the band's star signs: Leo (Roger), Leo (John), Virgo (Freddie) and Cancer (Brian). It was, of course, a damned good idea, and totally in tune with the flamboyant image of the band. It was a symbol that would first appear on the back of their first album, `Queen'. Armed with their regal backdrop, the band headed off for their first gig as `Queen'. Eighty of the expected one hundred and twenty guests turned up for a private viewing of the band at the College Of Estate Management, Hornsey, in June 1971.

Despite reports that Queen were, in fact, pretty awful that night - nervous and out of tune - the band were, in a small way, starting to gain confidence. With more and more gigs coming their way, they needed a reliable roadie, and found the perfect candidate in friend John Harris, who was to become an integral part of Queen's set-up as sound engineer. John's and Brian's girlfriends had been at the same college together. Other friends rallied around to help in other areas: P.A. technicalities, lighting and the sewing of their stage outfits (designed by Freddie, of course).

Queen were now including more and more of their own material in their repertoire, a sure sign that they were starting to believe in themselves and their songwriting ability. They no longer needed to lean on other people's songs for confidence, and they introduced such numbers as `Stone Cold Crazy' (which would appear on `Sheer Heart Attack') and `Liar' (included on the first album) and their special medley, which included `Jailhouse Rock'. Visually, each of the band was developing his own little characteristics, but none so obvious as Freddie's.

His days at college singing into a twelve-inch ruler, throwing his head back arrogantly and strutting about the gents' toilet, were beginning to pay off. He was playing it for real now, preening and posing with not a self-conscious bone in his body, appearing for all the world like some decadent, obscene, animal in a German stripjoint. A far cry from the unhappy immigrant boy who arrived in England twelve years earlier. Freddie was certainly making the most of his adopted country, and he would go on to bleed it dry in the years that followed...

In that first year, Queen played all over the place, but never in the usual clubs that other bands were appearing in. The `Queen circuit' comprised tiny colleges tucked away in odd places, dark corners where the band could develop without the restrictions (or embarrassments?) of playing before Joe Public. Thus nobody, in the press or general rock'n'roll public, really saw Queen coming!

Insidiously sneaking about just beneath the gaze of the public eye, the band were preparing for their ambush on the music business.

When college broke up for the summer holidays in July 1971, the band headed off for the South West again, this time to spend the entire two months touring the Cornwall area - care of Roger, naturally!

The band were, of course, spending more and more time away from home. Mr May recalls his impressions of the band at that time, and his concerns about the way his son's life was heading:

"We were a little worried at that stage that he

was spending so much time on music, although I think I was more worried about the effects of losing sleep and the crude travelling arrangements they had when they did go on those trips down to Cornwall. I think all parents worry about their childrens' safety, and it was nothing more than that.

"Brian was now staying in a flat in Barnes, and we used to sometimes drive round there with a change of clothes and things like that, and I remember us arriving there one afternoon and Brian introducing us to Roger and Freddie Mercury, and sitting there while they talked about all the plans they had for Queen. They were all wearing velvet jackets and flared trousers when they appeared on stage then, and they were discussing ideas for new stage clothes. They were a very close-knit band even then, but totally dissimilar people. Freddie was so extrovert, with very extravagant ways of expressing himself, whereas Brian was totally the opposite. But all of them had one thing in common - the pursuit of excellence."

Harold May's observations hit the nail firmly on the head and, as a comparative outsider, he could perhaps see a magic in the band that they, themselves, had not even seen. `Pursuit of excellence' was certainly the key to Queen's success.

Returning to London in September, Roger decided to leave the market stall for Freddie to run on his own - and he moved into a flat in Richmond whilst embarking on a Botany course at nearby Kew Gardens. Freddie meanwhile, still a massively devoted Jimi Hendrix fan, was distraught when his idol died on 18th September -

and closed the stall down for the day in respect (he would later close the stall down entirely, and start helping out on his friend, Alan Mair's, stall). Brian remembers Freddie's devotion to the great guitarist, and Hendrix' effect on a whole generation:

"More than any of us, Freddie was a manic Hendrix fan. I remember him going on and on about him. Then I saw Hendrix myself at one of Brian Epstein's shows where he supported The Who, and I remember thinking, this guy's so far in advance of everyone else. It was like he was on the same road that we were, but he was almost out of sight, ahead of us all! It was frightening and a bit upsetting really for us other guitarists. People are still trying to work out how he did all that stuff."

It was perhaps after Hendrix' death that all four members of Queen realised they'd all been heavily influenced by the most extraordinary guitarist to walk this earth, and that maybe it was Hendrix and Fate that had brought the band together in the first place!

During the last three months of the year, the band continued their round of college dates, culminating with a Rugby Club gig on New Year's Eve.

Queen had now spent almost a year paying their dues, but there was a light at the end of the seemingly endless tunnel of small gigs. In 1972, the band got their first unexpected break. Although most of Queen's rapidly-increasing circle of `contacts' were mainly hangers-on, Brian did have one bona fide business source.

Terry, a friend of Brian's, was working as an

engineer at Pye Studios, but was about to move to De Lane Lea Studios in Wembley. Chatting with Brian one day, he mentioned that De Lane Lea were searching for a band to test the suitability of equipment for dealing with the new `hard rock' music that was becoming more and more popular. The band would have to showcase their own material in front of potential clients of the studios.

Brian didn't hesitate. He told Terry to put the band's name forward immediately, and in early 1972, Queen eagerly bounced into De Lane Lea Studios, armed with a total belief that this was the break they'd been looking for.

Queen spent most of the first few months of 1972 taking advantage of this unique opportunity and, with the help of producer Louie Austin, recorded their material onto top-quality demos. Record companies' reaction to the resulting tapes was, however, apathetic, yet the band were enjoying themselves so much they hardly cared. But it's ironic to consider that the songs on these early demos would, in effect, become their debut album for EMI, one of the record companies who'd rejected the demos!

It was fascinating, and slightly overwhelming for this still wide-eyed band to be exposed to this up-to-the-minute equipment. But it wasn't just the equipment they were being exposed to.

A constant stream of respected production personnel would pass through the studios every day. It was a matter of course for them to check out the new facilities at De Lane Lea. Amongst these were two staff engineers from Trident Studios in Wardour Street, Roy Thomas Baker and John Anthony. Trident had seen, and would see the likes of David Bowie, Elton John and Carly Simon working under its roof.

John Anthony (who'd worked with Genesis and Van Der Graaf Generator) had, of course, already met the band, when he'd produced Smile's ill-fated `Earth' single at Trident in 1969.

While Roy Thomas Baker (who'd recently landed himself his first full-blown production job on Nazareth's second album) concentrated on studying the sound quality of Queen's tapes, John Anthony found himself more interested in the band's material itself. He was impressed to hear that the band, with the addition of Freddie and John, had progressed immeasurably since his experience with them. Baker, too, fell into the magic of Queen's music, and the two found themselves captivated with one song in particular, `Keep Yourself Alive'. Baker remembers that day:

"I thought it was fabulous, wonderful. I totally forgot about looking at the studio!"

Baker and Anthony returned to Trident's offices in Great Pulteney Street, London, bubbling with enthusiasm for their amazing `find'. They persuaded their employers, Norman and Barry Sheffield (managing directors of Centredisc, Trident's holding company) to investigate the band further. The Sheffields (who had considerable interests in the film industry and, of course, had their own studio complex) were, in any case, thinking of expanding their interests. They wanted to form their own record label primarily because of an interest in new singer, Eugene Wallace. Up until now, Trident was operating merely as a production company, recording artists like Ashton, Gardener and Dyke, and licensing the tapes through EMI, but now they wanted to handle the whole kaboosh themselves. However, in the midst of great speculation about the new Trident label, the Sheffields suddenly decided not to start the company. To this day, nobody really knows the reason for this abrupt turnabout. Wallace was, instead, presented with his own manager, American A&R dynamo Jack Nelson, who was brought in to guide his career. Nelson would later prove an interesting contributor to Queen's career...

In the Spring of 1972, Norman and Barry Sheffield quietly snuck off to Forest Hill Hospital where Queen were playing at the hospital's annual dance. They found themselves spellbound by the band's colourful image and dynamic repertoire.

Returning to Trident, they decided to sign Queen up immediately, and send them into the studio. The band were delighted, but it was to be a long time until those studio doors opened for them.

The group were still wary of business contracts, and they weren't entirely convinced that Trident were acting in their best interests. They were all business, promises, over-enthusiasm. Perhaps the Sheffields were putting too much emphasis on Queen's value as a potential money-making machine, and wanted to `own' them, rather than nurture and take pride in them as musicians.

So, in their infinite paranoia, the band scrutinised their contract laboriously, and demanded that certain clauses be included before signing on the dotted line. They insisted on having a management clause inserted, as well as agreements in respect of recording and production. Already, the seeds of `Queen Productions' were beginning to take root. The band, John in particular, were starting to think like businessmen - but only to ensure the very best representation for them and their music. Still, this was not the wisest of decisions, for they were tying themselves lock, stock and barrel to Trident if they signed a contract comprising management, recording and production clauses. The learning process was beginning...

The contract dissection, together with a great deal of procrastination on Trident's part, delayed studio work. Although the band were paid £100 per week from May, they didn't actually enter the studio until the end of the summer.

Because the Sheffields were aware that Queen might get tired of waiting, they decided to hunt out a manager/A&R man as soon as possible to keep them happy. On a trip to the States in June, Norman Sheffield visited his friend Jack Nelson at MGM to persuade him to handle Eugene Wallace - and to come over to England for a couple of years as Trident's much-needed A&R man and in-house manager. So far, John Anthony had been acting as Trident's A&R executive, on top of working as producer. Eager to kill two birds with one stone, Sheffield threw Queen into the conversation, and suggested to Nelson that, when he came to England to work on Wallace, he could, perhaps, work with Queen as well. Nelson agreed - and flew to England in June 1972.

Whether or not Queen knew of their new manager's involvement with Wallace, and that they were second priority on his and Trident's list, is open to speculation. Certainly, when they were only given `down-time' at the plush 24-track Trident Studios, it made them wonder about the Sheffields' faith in their music. The recording process, as such, was to be a long one, the band realised.

Still, they knew both Roy Thomas Baker and John Anthony believed in their abilities, and indeed the two engineers' motivation helped spur the band on through the sporadic recording process. It was a case of recording from 10.00am to 1.00pm, then returning at 4.00 the following morning. It was an unnerving experience for four musicians who prided themselves on their perfectionism. Jumping in and out of the studio at any given moment hardly gave them the opportunity to immerse themselves in creativity. So unsatisfactory were their attempts to record `The Night Comes Down' that it was the original version, from the De Lane Lea sessions, that landed on the album. Baker:

"It was a horrible way to record, but that's how the whole album came together."

Meanwhile, Baker had organised a showcase for Queen at The Pheasantry in the Kings Road, London. The event, on 6th November, was a total flop, the band failing to impress the exclusive audience of record company executives. But it was the band's first appearance under the cynical scrutiny of the business, and didn't affect Trident's decision to continue working with them. Queen were a naturally nervous band - they thrived on the adrenalin, it was part of their creative build-up.

At last contracts were exchanged between the two parties. Dave Thomas, working for Trident at the time, and later to become their co-manager, remembers his first impressions of Queen:

"When the band walked into the room, you just knew they were a class act. They were just a bunch of students, but they exuded this amazing charismatic energy - particularly Freddie. He was totally larger than life, quite awe-inspiring.

"But although the night at The Pheasantry (where I first saw them) was intended as a showcase, they bombed out completely. We'd invited all these different people along hoping that there'd be widespread interest in Queen, but the whole thing just didn't work. The noise was too much, and after that they were turned down by several companies."

When the band played their first gig as a signed band at the notorious Marquee Club on 20th December 1972, they were more confident. That `charismatic energy' powered into the stunned crowd, and it seemed that, at last, Queen were beginning to gain momentum as a live band. The magic was starting to take effect... Brian:

"Our stage act was a show, more rock'n'roll-orientated than the album actually, at that stage of the game. You can only get so far playing to audiences who don't understand what you're doing, so we did more accessible, heavy rock'n'roll with the Queen delivery to give people something they could get hold of - get on, sock it to 'em, get off!

"If you go on stage and people don't know your material, you can get boring if you do your own stuff all the time. So we did Bo Diddley's `I'm A Man', Elvis Presley's `Jailhouse Rock' and Little Richard's `Shout Bama Lama'. Give 'em a show, but don't make anything but the music your foundation."

In the background, the boys were still not convinced about the future Trident kept guaranteeing for them. After completing the album in December (at a cost of £13,000), each member veered off to their respective `off-shoot' careers, studies and part-time jobs. Freddie continued, on and off, to help on Alan Mair's stall, Roger was still studying Botany, John continued with his teaching job, and Brian followed suit by taking a job teaching Maths at a Stockwell comprehensive school. It was a case of make-or-break at this stage and Brian's oft-repeated catchphrase was:

"I am either going to get to the top - or chuck it!"

Whilst all living with a total determination that they were going to succeed on a massive scale, they each secretly held a realistic view of the situation. The odds, after all, were stacked against them.

Indeed, Jack Nelson was having a hard time selling the band to anyone. Armed with their 24-track demo and Freddie's shopping list of off-the-wall ideas for the band's presentation and image, Nelson could easily have given up. But, just when the going was getting tough, help arrived from the most unlikeliest of sources. `Queen' was about to see the light of day...or was it?

CHAPTER EIGHT

KILLER QUEEN
1973

*"We had quite a difficult genesis. It was very
difficult for us to get a contract, to be accepted in any
way. But many groups go through that, and it does
engineer a kind of `backs to the wall' feeling in a band.
So we felt very strong together."*
(Roger Taylor)

Contrary to speculation about Queen's `easy ride' to fame and fortune, they probably had more problems gaining serious credibility than most bands. The name, the image, the frustrating recording process - and the unbelievable delay in releasing `Queen' - all these factors weighed against the band during those first endless years. Not only that, but they were concerned about the public's image of their music. The last thing they wanted was to be represented by people who had no conception of the band's `modus operandi', and who might market them in the wrong way. It was frustrating trying to communicate their dreams to the business machine. They were beginning to wonder if perhaps they'd been foolish to leap at the first opportunity to present itself.

Still, there were people lurking in strange places who really did understand the magic and imagery of Queen...

The Midem Festival is held annually in the South Of France. A hustling, bustling community of music business people from all over the world, it is the scene of much wheeling, dealing and scrutiny. It is where, every January, a band should be represented by a shrewd manager whose only intention is to sign his property. A&R men, publishers, managers et al flock to the great music biz circus in search of raw talent, hoping to find the band of their dreams. Once in a blue moon, the right A&R man finds the right band, the chemistry works - and another page in rock'n'roll history is written...

Roy Featherstone, a top EMI executive, returned to London after his annual talent search at the 1973 Festival. He was exhausted. Listening to tape after tape of `appalling', `average' and `could be good' music was his job, but it was tedious, time-consuming and, most of the time, desperately frustrating. Featherstone had to be fussy, he couldn't just take any band from the above-average category and turn it into a `product' because he was fed up of listening to demos. He knew that somewhere there was a band who would fire his imagination, knock him back, make him want to take their music to the masses, and be proud of it.

He'd found that band at Midem, and had been so excited about their demo that he'd sent a telegram back to his staff in London urging them not to sign anything until he got back. Queen had hit him squarely between the eyes, and he was not about to let them slip through his fingers.

His first meeting back in London was with EMI label manager David Croker, one of the many executives who'd turned Queen down the previous summer. Croker listened to the demo again, and agreed with Featherstone that they should pursue the band. They both decided that Queen would be absolutely perfect for the new hard rock label EMI were about to launch.

Discovering, to their chagrin, that Queen were already signed to a production and management deal with Trident, Croker and Featherstone arranged a meeting with the company. EMI agreed to sign a distribution deal with Trident, and asked the production company to organise press and promotion. The band themselves were over the moon that one of the country's leading labels wanted to sign them. But it was at this point that they started to regret their liaison with Trident. They would have little say in negotiations - Trident, as their management, would be representing them to EMI. It was like having a noose round their necks. But there was a positive side. If EMI were prepared to deal with a middle-man to get to the band, then they were obviously serious about their intentions.

So the four excited, still green, musicians started to look forward to the unveiling of EMI's new label, cunningly titled `EMI'. Presuming that the album would be released shortly after the March launch, they started spreading the word. But it was not going to be that simple. In fact, what appeared to be the first confident step of their career turned out to be more of a stumble....

On 6th April 1973, David Croker issued an interdepartmental memo officially informing all EMI staff that the company were now handling the interests of an aspiring new rock band with the dubious name of `Queen'. The band would be playing a showcase (arranged by Trident) on 9th

April and, continued Croker, would any staff not doing anything that night kindly drag themselves down to the Marquee to check them out. A similar press release was circulated to the music papers. Thus the EMI publicity machine was beginning to grind away on Queen's behalf. Or not. The gig would prove to be the most ill-timed showcase in rock'n'roll history.

The band themselves were going through absolute hell. Nerves still jangling after their paranoic experience in the studio, they waited, day after day, for the news that `Queen' was about to reach the record shops. The Marquee gig was looming closer and closer, and the band were beginning to tear their hair out. Where was that bloody album?! What were EMI doing? What were Trident doing? Why the hell had they started this whole thing anyway?! They were angry, frustrated, disappointed and would, no doubt, have demanded the Marquee gig be pulled had they not been so eager to play live in front of such an exclusive audience. They were looking forward to the experience, and it couldn't do them any harm surely?

Queen exploded majestically onto the Marquee stage, startling everyone, including the EMI personnel, with a regal splash of the pompous `Procession'. The rest of the set followed suit - splendid, outrageous stuff! Freddie strutting arrogantly round the stage like a peacock on heat, Brian floating ethereally around in his own little bubble, John bobbing rhythmically, Roger thrashing wildly... It was a resoundingly successful gig, or so the band and everyone involved assumed.

The Reviews Pages were full of cynical, suspicious and damning words. The unspoken inference was `hype': that the band was purely a puppet band for EMI to play around with, to manufacture to their own specifications. And many journalists refused to see past the visual image which, of course, exploded around the focal point of the band - Freddie. His `campness' was, apparently, a deliberately-paraded, tasteless attempt to jump on the Bowie-Glitter-Bolan-Sweet-Slade bandwagon. Basically, Queen had already been written off as a bunch of `poofters', a somewhat prejudicial and inaccurate view. At that time, Freddie's bisexuality hadn't even become an issue. Indeed, he was as heterosexual as the next man, happily living with his girlfriend Mary Austin in their Holland Park flat. The campness was, at this stage, merely a reflection of Freddie's creative, artistic flair. He was using himself as a canvas - the visual ego of Queen's music, if you like. Black skin-tight catsuit, long black hair and fingernails, the overall effect was startling. A purring black panther prowling protectively around his domain.

The band were seen as a kind of parody of the macho hard rock bands around at the time: Led Zeppelin, Black Sabbath.... But it wasn't a deliberate parody, Queen were certainly not taking the piss. They were just proving that hard rock should be tailored to everyone's needs - male and female. But because of the femininity of their appearance - which incorporated the whole band, not just Freddie - they were, apparently, an unsavoury entity. Freddie's gamble, the image he'd perceived for the band in the summer of 1970, was not, apparently, paying off.

The rest of the band must've been wondering

why they'd gone along with this outrageous cockatoo's ideas in the first place.

Still, the press slating was nobody's fault but the record company's, who were to make matters worse by taking another three months to release the album. During that time, any momentum gained from the gig - it had, at least, started people talking - was lost.

Then, out of the blue, Trident Audio stuck their oar in as well.

The bizarre gimmick of a single they released in June 1973 could've proved to be the final straw for Queen's stumbling career. It was yet another sign that the company were apparently either desperately greedy or incredibly stupid - certainly they had a rare talent for bad-timing. Luckily, nobody found out until much later that `Larry Lurex', who sang on the cover of the Spector-penned `I Can Hear Music' was none other than Freddie Mercury! It would've done Queen no end of damage to've been publicly involved, just before the release of their own single and album, with such a dire Gary Glitter-style project. The Glitter fan club were, apparently, up in arms over this obvious piss-take. Fortunately the single, which had been a Top Ten hit for The Beach Boys in 1969, died a death. Freddie was more than a little relieved, and the whole band were only too glad to sweep the episode under the carpet. A close shave at a time when Queen were already walking tightropes...

Trident had acted in the most unprofessional way but, at the moment, the band had to stick with the company, however much they wished they had direct contact with EMI.

So how had the Larry Lurex `project' come about? Certainly, Queen had not deliberately recorded a session for producing as a single. No, it was all a product of a low-key experiment.

Robin Geoffrey Cable was one of Trident's producers who, at the time Queen were in Trident Studios recording `Queen', was carrying out a production experiment. Cable was attempting to recreate the revolutionary `Phil Spector sound', using the Beach Boys' `I Can Hear Music' (Greenwich, Spector and Barry) as his guinea-pig. Freddie, Brian, Roger and John, during their many breaks in recording, would spend most of their spare time hanging around the studios waiting for their next period of down-time. One day, Cable called Freddie into his studio to help with the experiment, claiming that he had just the right vocal sound for the Spector test. As Brian and Roger happened to be around as well, they pitched in too. So theoretically, `I Can Hear Music' could have been Queen's first single had John Deacon chipped in too! Obviously, the band didn't think anything would come of it. Indeed, by the time the Larry Lurex single emerged, they'd forgotten all about it.

The single, which had a cover of Dusty Springfield's `Goin' Back' on the flip-side, wasn't actually that bad - it was more the image that appalled people. Though a far cry from Queen's usual work, Freddie's lisping vocals worked well against the wall-of-sound backdrop, Brian's guitar and Roger's drumming no insult to their talents. But obviously such a number was nothing to do with Queen or the image they were trying to put across. Had it been revealed too early that they were, in fact, `Larry Lurex', the consequences could've been disastrous.

A month after Larry Lurex slithered into obscurity, Queen's planned single, the May-composed `Keep Yourself Alive' (B-side `Son And Daughter', also written by Brian), was released, followed a week later, on 13th July 1973, by the album. Unfortunately, the general reaction to `Queen' was nothing for the band to get excited about. Because of the yawning gap between Marquee gig and album release, EMI had felt it necessary to lavish as much commercial pressure as possible on the release. But the overbloated promotional blitz merely heightened the press' convictions that Queen were no more than a record company hype. Their glorious career had certainly started on the wrong foot. Through no fault of their own, they'd managed to put the press' backs up - the very people who they needed to impress at this stage. Their record company's, and production company's, shortcomings were reflecting on the band, and it galled them. Roger: "It's rubbish to say we were hyped. We started playing the really small gigs, and then we released an album. There was no particularly big splash of publicity or anything... Now Cockney Rebel - their publicity came before they'd done anything."

Freddie was more objective, but equally annoyed: "I think, to an extent, we're a sitting target, because we gained popularity quicker than most bands and we've been talked about more than any other band in the last month, so it's inevitable. Briefly, I'd be the first one to respect fair criticism. I think it would be wrong if all we got were good reviews, but it's when you get unfair, dishonest reviews where people haven't done their homework that I get annoyed."

It was only the mixed reviews for the single - some of which actually praised the band - that kept them going. It was just a shame the album hadn't received the same kind of attention. Some of the better reviews for `Keep Yourself Alive' went like this:

`A raucous, but still well-built single. The vocal interchanges make it stand out in a rather crowded week. Good power from behind, but the vocal depths make it.' (Record Mirror)

`This really is one of the best singles of the year, and ought to set the gracious Queen on the road to success. The more I play it, the more I am convinced it has everything a hit single needs - without being overtly commercial. The guitar work is fast, precise and ear-catching, and the vocal refrain will keep coming back and hitting you after the first hearing.' (Birmingham Mail)

`This is a marching, charging band that will soon be making headlines in the sledgehammer and boots variety of rock. Young, beautiful, possessed of demonic rock and roll fire - what more could a fan craving pin-ups and urging to unleash total devotion ask for in a group? Nothing of course, and the hell-fire sounds of Queen could be rocketing from speakers everywhere before the summer is over.' (Middlesex Times)

The more cynical critics wrote grudgingly:

`Queen's press release hastens to add that Queen are a minor sensation, stunningly visual, etc. Doubtless, they're kind to their parents and dumb animals too; beneath those shiny showbiz exteriors they're regular guys (former scouts and graduate meals-on-wheels moguls). This genteel refrain kicks off (a popular expression dans le business) with a

*scrubbing, phased rhythm guitar, joined by an
attractively stilted, vaguely Hendrixy lead riff merging
into the body (or outer casing) of the tune, a tromping,
chordy, early Who-style passage with frantic white-boy
vocals, and a drum solo that'd make Dave Clark's day.
It should do well.'* (Disc)

`If these guys look half as good as they sound, they
could be huge. But that name threatens more
Roxy/Bowie/Sweet gay games, which not only wind up
distracting the musicians from playing music, but are
going out of fashion. The sound goes back past Roxy to
The Who and the Electric Prunes, using moog as
music, not just sound effects, managing to make the
scattershot lyrics mean something. Good singer, cleanly
recorded. Do us all a favour, fellas, change your name
to the Uncouth and go on stage in jock-straps.'*
(Melody Maker)

Had the latter critic not noted the `disclaimer'
on the album sleeve: `...and nobody played
synthesiser'?

However flattering some of the reviews may've
been, there were plenty of other,
uncomplimentary and inaccurate reviews. One
critic compared Queen to the New York Dolls, a
band who hadn't yet been exposed to Britain, and
sounded nothing like the band. Another insisted
on calling John Deacon `Deacon John'! The general
vibe from the press was ignorance and contempt.
From the critics' point of view, the band had been
hyped to the hilt, and had a lot of dues to pay to
change the mass media's mind. It was to be a long
time before that happened. The press stoically
insisted that the band had appeared from
nowhere, refusing to acknowledge that they had,
in fact, been `paying their dues' for over three
years.

This attitude was one that would become a major feature of Queen's entire career. A case of Queen versus The Press. At this stage, they cared deeply about criticism, and it was only the more flattering reviews that helped them learn to live with those cutting comments. The learning process continued...

But it wasn't just the press who were giving Queen a hard time. Radio One, in typically arrogant fashion, rejected `Keep Yourself Alive' no less than five times. Even Capital Radio's and Alan Freeman's willingness to stick their necks out didn't save it from disappearing into Neverneverland. Both album and single failed to chart. Queen were regarded as nothing more than either a commercial regurgitation of the fashionable hard rock sound, or a poor, unfashionable glamrock band. It all seemed very unfair, but predictable really.

EMI had overdone the £5000 publicity campaign, thrusting this unknown band forcibly in everyone's faces, with free copies of the album and single bandied about as incentive. So it should have been foreseen that the reception would be one of suspicion. EMI ought to have, firstly, released the album (or at least the single) to coincide with the Marquee gig and, secondly, toned down promotional activities. Queen's music would've spoken for itself, instead of being drowned out by unnecessarily loud publicity. After all, if a band is given the red carpet welcome before they've really earnt it, they're bound to come up against derision. Queen did not yet deserve such pomp and circumstance.

In retrospect, with their collective business acumen, the band could've set up their own low-key Queen organisation right from the beginning. More club gigs, a slowly-increasing cult following, circulation of demos to the press, live reviews as an unsigned band: gradual build-up of reputation and respect.

That way, when the band finally signed a major deal, at least a solid reputation would've preceded them, instead of record company hearsay. It's easy to say this now, of course, and in any case, after Queen's early hiccups...well, the rest is history!

A month after the album's release, the band were back in Trident Studios with Roy Thomas Baker and Robin Cable. They were despondent at first about the realities they'd had to face up to, but the spirit was still very much alive. Now, at least, they had their own studio time. Scenes from the down-time sessions of the first album were always fraught with tension - flying plates and cups, a great deal of effing and blinding. This time, the tension was not so great. They had the chance to get their teeth into the meat of creativity in a much more relaxed atmosphere.

Perhaps they'd grown up in the last six months as well. The songs that were to comprise `Queen II' hinted at a tougher attitude than their previous material.

As they sunk themselves into their bubble of creativity, disappearing gratefully from the public eye, so the pressure of criticism receded. Indeed, as the press discovered that Queen were back in the studio, resolutely forging onwards rather than scampering off like wounded animals, their cynicism waned a little. So it *was* a record company cock-up after all.

Help was heading the band's way too, from people who truly believed in the Queen magic. The Johnstone sisters and Tony Brainsby were to play a large part in Queen's future...

Pat and Sue Johnstone had been brought up near Truro, where Roger Taylor went to school. They originally met him through his girlfriend, whom they'd often hang around with, and soon became close friends with Roger too. The sisters were both involved with music - indeed, Sue sang regularly in a local folk club. Pat moved to London around the same time Roger started his Dentistry course, first working as a nanny and later taking up her own stall in Kensington Market alongside Roger and Freddie. Sue followed her sister to the big city lights a year later, after her band Wizard had folded. Pat recalls the hustle and bustle of the market in the early days:

"There was a great atmosphere. We were all involved in it together and it was work and social life all combined. It was a coming-together of musicians and artists who all had something in common through the market."

The Johnstones got to know the band so well that it was decided, in the summer of 1973, that they should be responsible for handling the Queen Fan Club. Trident were beginning to show a certain dedication to the band by now, as it was they who financed the fan club - and they had, by September 1973, invested a total of £62,000 in the band. But still, there was no excuse for the mistakes they had made along the way. Differences of opinion still occur over Trident's attitude in those early days - an attitude that would finally lead to a severance of ties...

The Fan Club took a while to get started. First, the sisters had to settle into their offices at Trident, then there was the merchandise to sort out. But fan club members were joining thick and fast, at the ridiculous fee of 50p a year. The first newsletter was basic - that the band were working on their second album, and that: `In return for this vast sum (50p), you will receive the usual goodies, such as t-shirts, badges, stickers and posters.'

It was a fairly amateurish affair to start with, but when the Johnstones got into the swing of it, there was no stopping them. Eventually, they had large stocks of flash membership cards to send out to members, printed in gold on a black background with the band's logo - Freddie's birthsign emblem. Stationery, stickers and transfers followed suit. Every now and then, the band would each write their own personal letter to their fans. The fan club started as a self-supporting, friendly little organisation, which gradually grew into the massive, all-encompassing network it is today.

As the club started to blossom, Trident decided to haul in a professional publicist to handle Queen's ever-expanding promotional needs.

Tony Brainsby was one of the top publicists at the time, whose client list included the likes of Paul McCartney and Cat Stevens. His right-hand man at the time was John Bagnall who, by a strange quirk of fate, was to become label manager at EMI. Brainsby was brought in by Jack Nelson, and with his natural instinct for publicity, he set to work on the band's image. It was difficult at first. He had to overcome the band's reputation for being a `supermarket rock' band, a contrived hype. One music paper in particular was refusing to have anything to do with the band, dismissing them as nothing more than a `bunch of poofters'.

Brainsby worked closely with the band from the start, impressed by their single-minded ideas for their own image. But the one aspect that struck him above all else was how different Queen looked compared to the popular rock bands around at the time. Whilst the fashion amongst most groups was to dress in t-shirts and jeans (Status Quo being the leader of that particular trend), Queen's style was much more sophisticated, chic-er and sleeker. The band walked into his office - and Brainsby knew instinctively that these guys were going to be stars. Freddie in blue silk jacket and white trousers, Roger with long blonde hair falling over beautifully-embroidered jacket, Brian dressed head-to-toe in black velvet, John in black silk suit. The effect was startling. But, observed Brainsby, there was nothing camp about the band, an aspect he was expecting to have to 'discuss' with the boys. `Camp' was a media invention, but one which Freddie would greatly enjoy playing up to.

Brainsby listened to them, and built his promotional campaign out of their own modus operandi, after discovering that these boys were not only talented, but intelligent. He knew his job was not to invent stories about the band for sensationalism, but to enhance and project what was already there. A kind of medium between band, press and public.

Accordingly, the press' attitude did soften a little, which made it easier for the band to concentrate on their music. But they would always remain in close contact with Brainsby, ensuring they had plenty of say over publicity matters. It was they who would sift through photos taken by their regular photographer, Mick Rock, rejecting those they didn't like, and deciding which shots should be used.

As well as recording the album, Queen were also raising their profile as a live band. The last quarter of the year was riddled with gigs here and there, and these would lead up to the group's biggest live break to date at the end of the year.

TV and radio companies finally seemed to be cottoning on to the band's genuine talent. It seemed that the media, in general, were coming to their senses, and opening their doors to the band.

On 13th September 1973, they played their first recorded gig at Golders Green Hippodrome for broadcasting on Radio Luxembourg the following month, timed to coincide with their forthcoming visit. Freddie, in particular, was in his element posing about in front of the camera, displaying his penchant for exhibitionism. Later on that same day, they returned to The Imperial College for a good-humoured, relaxed gig in front of the students they knew so well. 24th September, and `Whispering' Bob Harris introduced Queen to his `Sounds Of The Seventies' radio show. On 1st October, Trident shot a promotional film of Queen, including a rendition of `Keep Yourself Alive' for use on a future `Old Grey Whistle Test'. Life was getting disturbingly busy!

From 11th to 14th October, the band took in their first `TV tour' of Europe, for television appearances in Belgium, France and Holland, culminating with gigs in Germany and Luxembourg (at Le Blow Up). Returning to England, they discovered that the BBC were finally seeing sense - about time - and, on 20th October, they were filmed live at the Paris Theatre, London, for a forthcoming `In Concert' session for Radio One.

But all this was only the beginning. As the end of the year drew closer, Queen were offered the opportunity of a life-time: a support tour with Mott The Hoople, currently scoring high in the charts with `All The Way From Memphis'. Trident had been responsible for clinching this much sought-after opportunity. After making the promotional film, they'd decided to use it to circulate to business contacts. One of these was Bob Hirschman, an old friend of the Sheffields, who also happened to manage Mott. He agreed that, as long as Trident paid for Queen's P.A. and lighting, the band could have the tour.

As a prelude to that tour, Queen played a one-off, sold-out gig at Imperial on 2nd November, and it was generally reckoned that the band had improved beyond all expectations.

The tour itself started on 12th November 1973 at Leeds Town Hall, continuing through to 14th December, where Queen were confronted by the notorious Hammersmith Odeon crowd for the first time. The whole experience had been a roaring success, creatively if not commercially, the band earning standing ovations time after time for their extraordinary repertoire, which was now including numbers off the `Queen II' album. `Procession' had been opening their set for a long time now, but the band were gradually trickling in a few more new numbers.

The Hammersmith Odeon gigs were particularly memorable. On the first night, the band turned up late onstage, and caused a riot between both bands' roadcrews! When Mott The Hoople had to overrun their set, the Odeon management decided to lower the safety curtain to cut the show short. Hoople's reaction? To push their keyboard in the curtain's path, so that it couldn't be lowered all the way to the stage-floor! It was all part of the fun of rock'n'roll, although at the time obviously, the incident wasn't funny at all.

Reviews of Queen's appearances were mixed. As usual, the band had to put up with those occasional, but incredibly scathing comments, the worst being from their constant adversary, Melody Maker, who dribbled:

`Queen were rather disappointing with a chilly, gutless sound that just didn't project itself off stage. No one number was distinctive, except perhaps `Liar'.'

Of course, it hadn't dawned on any of their critics how much physical pain Queen were going through for their art, particularly Freddie. Tony Brainsby had first seen the band at the Marquee in 1972, followed swiftly by a "strange gig" at a Basingstoke girls' school dance. He remembered going backstage after that event, and how appalled he'd been at the bruising Freddie'd sustained banging his tambourine on his leg throughout the gig. He was physically exhausted and in obvious pain. But this was just the way the band operated - they loved their art, and they would, literally, go through hell and high water, including the media's ignorance, to achieve ultimate success.

Whatever, the press' customary slagging didn't deter the MAM booking agency from offering

Queen their own headline tour, an offer that the band regarded as almost predictable. Freddie:

"The responsibility now lies with us. But I've always thought of us as a top group. Sounds very big-headed, I know, but that's the way it is. The opportunity of playing with Mott was great, but I knew darn well the moment we finished that tour, as far as Britain was concerned we'd be headlining."

Mott The Hoople themselves were so impressed by their support band's behaviour (the Odeon gig was obviously just a case of end-of-tour over-zealousness!) that they invited Queen to join them on their Stateside tour the following Spring.

In less than a year, Queen had risen from a `contrived hype' that nobody believed in, to an extraordinary, outrageous talent capable of giving their own headline band a run for their money...

Everything was progressing so smoothly, what could possibly go wrong?

CHAPTER NINE

KEEP YOURSELF ALIVE
1974

Sickness, set-backs - and success

1974 started with a bang, certain music papers abruptly sussing that the band they most loved to hate was, in reality, about to make the big splash. The evidence was overwhelming, and Sounds and the NME, in particular, had to grudgingly accept Queen's popularity. The band had featured heavily in the 1973 Sounds Readers' Poll, coming third in the `Best New British Band' section and ninth in the `Best New International Artist' category. In the NME's poll, they were voted second `Most Promising Band', beneath Leo Sayer.

So, bowing under reader pressure, the press predictably decided to cover Queen more extensively. Suddenly, the story of Brian's `Red Special' and its construction was splashed across double-page spreads in all the popular music papers. The whole band were being sought after for `exclusive' interviews. Details of the band's academic qualifications, profiles of each member, including Freddie's alleged `gayness' (well, if he would run around saying things like "I'm as gay as a daffodil"...), were now of great importance, and highly topical. Every music journalist was claiming to be the one who'd discovered the band first. A remarkable change of heart...

But, no sooner had the press started to

insipidly smile upon the group, than their opinion ceased to be relevant anymore. The poll results had made Queen realise that it was the public who'd brought all this media attention their way, and that without their fans, there would be no band. Needless to say, the printed word ceased to wound the band anymore. Criticism was now a laughing matter, praise welcome but unimportant.

The band's new-found confidence reflected in their stage performances. Their gigs were really starting to become `shows', they wanted their audiences to enjoy the spectacle of watching them, not just listening to them. It was a sign of the spectacular presentations that would become Queen's trade mark.

In February 1974, playing their first gigs of the year at, of all places, the three-day Sunbury Music Festival in Melbourne, Australia, they started to display real star quality. They'd always lived, and played, on their nerves, but now it was a case of feeding on those nerves for adrenalin. They were definitely high - but on their own exhilaration, nothing synthetic. Brian:

"It's when I see everyone waving their hands and stamping their feet and generally moving around that I think back to just a few years ago. No-one knew us then and nothing was really happening. The music was there, it's just the audiences who make the difference.

"The difference between playing a sound-check and playing in front of a live audience proves it. There's a world of difference in the way you feel about the way you're playing. It's the audience that does it."

Queen returned to England after their few days' down-under to find a fleet of photographers waiting for them at the airport. Surely their profile hadn't risen that fast? Freddie, of all of them, certainly believed the band deserved such treatment. But, alas, it was not to be. The paparazzi had turned up to greet *the* Queen! When they realised their mistake, that it was only `Britain's Biggest Unknowns' (as Sounds had splashed across their paper), they left in disgust. Charmant. Only a few weeks later, said photographers would be kicking themselves for not grabbing the opportunity of capturing the latest hot Top Ten band...

`Seven Seas Of Rhye', conceived by Freddie, said it all. The single, released on 25th February 1974 as a taster for the forthcoming second album, was everything Queen represented. Freddie's gamble was, after all, starting to show dividends. The song was intense but catchy, heavy yet with enough pop to entertain the chart-going public. It was a combination of Led Zeppelin and Yes - yet sounded distinctly different to everything else that was currently cluttering up the charts. The New Seekers, Mud, Suzi Quatro, all those bands faithfully keeping within certain `glitterati' borders, suddenly looked rather outdated.

`Seven Seas Of Rhye' (a new lengthier version than the one on the first album) entered the charts at number 45 on 9th March. Nobody, the press and band alike, could believe what was happening to them. Sounds was aghast at such an innovative release - and positively oozed with unexpected praise:

`Taken from the forthcoming `Queen II' LP... I like Queen for their excess and their craziness although *cynical friends have described them as `Sweet gone heavy'. By their own standards this single is pretty restrained although there's some crunching guitar to be heard and enjoyed. Piano opens the song and the lyrics seem to concern themselves with some bloke who shuffles in from outer-space to run the show down here. As I understand it he's a pretty easy-going sort of chap - until you cross him and then he jumps on you from a great height. I may have got most of that wrong so don't believe it implicitly. A lot takes place musically as the tale of derring-do unfurls, there are some high harmonies that'll give your cat sleepless nights, guitars roar and thunder and a good time is to be had by all. Just as you think the lyrics are becoming a shade Moody Blues-ish you find that Queen, God bless 'em, have moved somehow into `I Do Like To Be Beside The Seaside'. Could even ease its way into the lower reaches. Hope so.'*

This particular writer was, of course, correct about the effect the single would have on the charts and, subsequently, the nation.

Queen's appearance on Top Of The Pops was extraordinary - and unexpected. Because a David Bowie promotional film hadn't arrived in time for the show, Queen were hauled in at the last minute to play live. The effect on the record-buying public was unprecedented. Millions of TV viewers, expecting to see the usual throwaway pop songs on their favourite show, widened their eyes in amazement at the outrageous sight before them. The singer, hair falling like a sheet of black liquid round startling Persian features, was the most pompous frontman anyone had ever seen. Stalking around the stage in black head-to-toe catsuit, black nail varnish glistening in the hot studio lights, the decadent young animal tossed his head back and stared in arrogant appraisal of his `subjects' in the audience. Freddie had suddenly become the most dangerous singer in the business - his parents must've truly thought he was the Devil himself by now! At the time, he remarked on his image:

"The black silk and leather influence comes from visiting a number of bars in Germany. Of course, I wear it with panache..."

More recently, he commented: "When I look back on all that black nail varnish and stuff, I think, `God, what did I do?' I used to feel a need for all that on stage. It made me feel more secure."

`Seven Seas Of Rhye' abruptly rose to No 10, and the snowball effects started almost immediately. EMI were getting it right this year - in conjunction with Queen's full-scale headline tour, `Queen II' was released (on 8th March). By the time it landed on the record shop shelves the band, supported by Nutz, were only four barnstorming gigs into the tour.

The first show at Blackpool Winter Gardens nearly didn't happen at all, when the band's lighting van broke down miles from the venue. But Fate was just playing a joke on them, and in the end they went onstage on time. The tour rolled onwards, the band grabbing handfuls of new fans along the way. When they kept the crowd waiting at Plymouth Guildhall on 3rd March, the chanting began. The group couldn't believe what they were hearing as they hastily tuned up backstage: `God Save The Queen!' the audience sang heartily as they waited for their favourite band. It was the start of a regular feature at Queen gigs throughout their career.

The album too was gaining momentum and, by the end of March, `Queen II' was sitting pretty at No 5. EMI, somewhat peeved that Queen's overseas record company, Elektra, had succeeded in selling their debut album more effectively than them (130,000 copies sold in the U.S. without the band even visiting the country), re-released `Queen' at the same time. It subsequently reached No 24, a sign that the group were fast becoming 1974's favourite band.

As the album poured out of the record shops, so the fans poured into Queen's gigs. Such was their exuberance for their new-found heroes that, at Stirling University on 16th March, a mass riot broke out. When the band failed to turn up for a fourth encore, the crowd's disappointment nearly ended in tragedy when two members of the audience were stabbed, and two crew members injured. The following night's gig at Barbarella's in Birmingham was subsequently postponed until 2nd April, to follow a sold-out gig at the Rainbow, London on 31st March. Originally, the band hadn't wanted to play the legendary (and now non-existent) rock'n'roll theatre, dubious as they were about filling the place. But promoter Mel Bush assured them that they would have no problems - and, sure enough, all tickets sold out a week in advance. It had been a worthwhile, but very tough tour for such a comparatively fledgling band. Freddie:

"It was a heavy tour, but it put us in a different bracket overnight. It's a tour we had to do, and I think now we've done it, we can do the next British tour on our own terms, exactly how we like.

"With this tour, we were booked in well beforehand at semi-big venues and, by the time we came to doing them, we had the album out, we'd got a bit of TV exposure and everything escalated. I think if we'd waited we could have done all the big venues - it's just a matter of timing. But I'm glad we did the tour when we did, even though there was a lot of physical and mental strain - so many things to worry about other than the music."

Meanwhile, reviews of the album had been the usual mixture of the complimentary and the derogatory: `This is it, the dregs of glamrock. The band with the worst name have capped that dubious achievement by bringing out the worst album for some time. Their material is weak and overproduced. The Black Side (literally!) is penned by vocalist Freddie Mercury, while the White Side, except for `Loser In The End' is written by guitarist Brian May. That track, written by drummer Roger Taylor, must be the worst piece of dross every committed to plastic - like `She's Leaving Home' meets Black Sabbath? As a whole, it is dire, while the musicianship isn't a lot better. Brian May is technically proficient but Freddie Mercury's poor voice is dressed up with multi-tracking. The rhythm section is fairly good. A lot of people are pushing Queen as the band of `74. If this is our brightest hope for the future then we are committing rock and roll suicide.' (Record Mirror)

Melody Maker claimed that the album sounded `over-complicated for their musical abilities' and that the group was `a cold fish'! The NME advised them to `cut this aura of self-laudatory crap', but Disc was more complimentary, declaring correctly that `Queen II' was `going to be a hit album'.

Whatever the press said, Queen were on a rollercoaster - everything was happening for them at the same time: both albums and a single riding high in the charts, their first headline tour a creative and financial success. And now they had the six-week American Mott The Hoople tour to look forward to...

Flying out to the States on 15th April 1974, Queen embarked on their greatest challenge yet, but a month into the tour disaster struck. The band had trekked from Denver, Colorado, through Kansas, Missouri, Oklahoma, Tennessee, Massachusetts, Rhode Island, Oregon, Pennsylvania, Connecticut - and had just completed a week at the Uris Theatre, Broadway, New York when Brian May was struck down with hepatitis. Freddie:

"When he turned yellow, we thought he had food poisoning..."

Queen were replaced by Kansas on the rest of the tour, much to their severe disappointment, and on 16th May, Brian was flown back to London for treatment, where he spent four weeks in hospital. Hepatitis is a quarantine disease in the States that requires the sufferer to leave the country immediately. The rest of the band, and anyone else who'd come into close contact with Brian, hastily inoculated themselves. Sadly, the hepatitis was to become a recurring feature of Brian's life.

So, just when their career had really started to take off, they were forced to land again. Buzzing with adrenalin, enough energy to keep working for the rest of the year, but they had to sit back and wait for Brian to regain his health. It was horribly frustrating - and Brian himself felt guilty, irrationally of course. But he was aware that his illness had affected the whole band, and that made him feel angry at himself.

Brian's health didn't fully return at all that year. Just when he was beginning to recover, and the band were looking forward to their own U.S. tour in the Autumn, he was taken ill again - this time with a duodenal ulcer. On 2nd August, he was rushed to hospital again and, for a second time, the band's plans were thwarted.

Still, they realised, even if they couldn't play live, they did at least have ample opportunity to start planning the next album. After Brian's recovery from his hepatitis attack in May, they'd spent a month rehearsing songs for the next album, then immersed themselves in Trident Studios on 15th July to start recording. Even after Brian's second illness, Queen assured their British fans that they'd still be able to gig around the country later in the year.

The six-month hibernation could've been the death of Queen - but, in fact, it had entirely the opposite effect. As far as their fans were concerned, it was a case of `absence makes the heart grow fonder'. `Seven Seas Of Rhye' had made sufficient impact to maintain the band's profile for a good few months.

That period also gave Brian time to appraise his life, and he decided it was time to put aside his thesis for the foreseeable future. This was a theory shared by John Deacon who, similarly optimistic about Queen's future, had recently given up his teaching job. It wasn't that the band were now earning enough that they didn't need their day jobs anymore - on the contrary, they were all, as Brian remembers: "...penniless, you know, just like any other struggling rock'n'roll band. All sitting around London in bedsitters, just like the rest." They just didn't have the time for anything else but the band.

Brian also found he had a unique opportunity to think about the way the whole band's career was shaping up and, during his convalescence, he managed to arrange the band's next British tour in November, and to plan all their personal promotion. He was becoming a finely-tuned businessman, as well as virtuoso musician and scientist!

The recording process for `Sheer Heart Attack', much like that of the first album, was sporadic because Brian's illnesses meant he could only work intermittently. When he did manage to come into the studio, his contributions were so below-par they had to be scrapped. So it was decided that he would write in hospital or at home, and that when he was well enough he could overdub his guitar parts.

Against all odds, the album - recorded at Rockfield Studios in Monmouth, Air Studios and Trident with Roy Thomas Baker - was completed within three months, to a standard acceptable to everyone. Brian: "For some strange reason, we seemed to get rather a different feel on `Sheer Heart Attack' because of the way we were forced to record it, and even allowing for all the problems we had, none of us were really displeased with the final result."

As usual, Brian was understating the facts! `Sheer Heart Attack' turned out to be their toughest, rockiest, most emphatic album ever. And it was to be their highest-charting album to date when it was released in October, climbing to a staggering No 2 on 1st November 1974. In America and Japan, it sat comfortably in the Top Ten for a good few weeks.

But, even before that third album was released, `Queen II' was earning its own rewards. By September, it had reached the £75,000 sales mark and, on 5th September at the Café Royale in London, they were presented with a Silver disc. The press reception was their first appearance in public since that forced summer recess (apart from Roger and John's visit to the EMI/Radio Luxembourg car rally at Brands Hatch on 11th August), and the event was ample evidence that their popularity hadn't waned in the least. The award was presented, in true music business style, by Jeanette Charles, the Queen's lookalike, who delivered the following Brainsby-penned speech in typically regal style:

`Ladies and Gentlemen, it gives me great pleasure to present Queen with this silver disc for 250,000 sales of their LP `Queen II'. I understand that over the past few months the band has suffered a setback with Brian May's illnesses. I am so glad to see that he is now fully recovered and back working with the band on their new LP and single. I unfortunately missed the band's appearance at The Rainbow earlier this year. However, I look forward to seeing them later this autumn when they begin their tour in November. Thank you.'

On 11th October, Queen's third single was released. `Killer Queen' (a double `A' side with `Flick Of The Wrist'), from the forthcoming album, rocketed to No 2, impeded from the top of the charts only by David Essex's `I'm Gonna Make

You A Star'. Freddie received an Ivor Novello award for composing the song which, he explained in no uncertain terms, was about "...a high-class call girl. I'm trying to say that classy people can be whores as well!". The award, and the single's lofty chart position, immediately rubbished the following Melody Maker review. That particular music paper appeared to be the only one who hadn't cottoned on to Queen's obvious potential:

> ``Killer' tries very hard to be sophisticated and intelligent, but merely substitutes a tasteless and not very clever manipulation of standard images for those qualities. By slicking up the production with all kinds of vocal effects and phrasing, Queen hope you won't notice how dreadful the song actually is. It's almost as dire as `Flick', which has the band attempting to sound vicious and menacing, with another set of frightfully inept lyrics. Listening to this record is like staring into the dark.'

Brian summed up the relief the band felt when the single near-as-dammit hit the jackpot:"`Killer Queen' was the turning point. It was the song that best summed-up our kind of music, and a big hit, and we desperately needed it as a mark of something successful happening for us."

Indeed. The band had made one helluva `comeback', categorically establishing themselves with a single and an album simultaneously at No 2. To emphasise their almighty splash into the music business, their publishers, Feldmans, gave them a specially-engraved tankard on 18th October to celebrate their success throughout Britain and America.

But there was more to come. The long-awaited

headline tour began on 30th October, neatly coinciding with the album's release and the single's continuing success. Starting at Manchester Palace Theatre and supported by Hustler, the band's progress on the tour was predictable. `Killer Queen' they were indeed! At Liverpool and Leeds University on 1st and 2nd November, the band were greeted by hysterical crowds storming the stage. When the bouncers pitched in to `sort out' the situation Freddie, on both nights, stopped the gig to calm everyone down. He succeeded - the press reports were laced with a grudging admiration for the band's responsibility to their fans, and the obvious affinity between Queen and their audience. Even the few journalists who slated the tour wrote their reviews with a kind of bewildered respect. One such reviewer was Chris Charlesworth:

`It is only fair to point out that my view of the concert appeared to be that of the minority and the majority went home satisfied.'

Their stage-show had been developing as a visual feast over the years, but on this particular tour, the sheer dynamics were really beginning to swell. The physical burden of their light and sound equipment, coupled with the vast dimensions of their ever-growing stage panorama, demanded the use of a forty-foot articulated truck, a ten-ton lorry and a fifteen-man roadcrew. Not forgetting the chauffeur-driven limousine for the musicians themselves, of course. Queen were, literally, expanding. They were also becoming much more finicky about their work, insisting on a mighty two-and-a-half-hour soundcheck before each show to ensure a perfect sound.

Freddie, in particular, was insistent that they concentrate heavily on the visual drama of their stage performance. Part of the reason for this, he was to reveal later, compensated for his onstage insecurity - to smother himself in image. Zandra Rhodes, who'd been designing their stage-clothes for a couple of years, created a new set of elaborate costumes for them under Freddie's instructions - a selection of floating silk affairs that accentuated the feline side of the band.

Their set would open with the stage in pitch dark, a single spotlight picking out Freddie's solitary figure as he sang the opening bars to `Now I'm Here', before the rest of the band burst into the main body of the song. Time and time again, the audience reaction was overwhelming - and at Glasgow Apollo, the manager presented Queen with a silver statuette for selling out his venue, a rarity by all accounts. That particular show had, in fact, almost ended in disaster. The front row's excitement had resulted in Freddie being dragged into the audience clutching his mike lead. The damage was excessive - more than any gig had caused in at least three or four years - with the first ten rows of seats completely decimated. Yet, for the Apollo, it was the best thing that'd happened to them in years!

Ending the tour on a particularly high note, the band played two resounding gigs at The Rainbow. The second night had to be added when, as with the rest of the tour, the first was sold out in two days. The final night, on 20th November, was filmed for a forthcoming cinema screening 'Queen at The Rainbow'. It was a particularly triumphant night, the response amazing, with the audience screaming for their favourite numbers - `Liar', `Keep Yourself Alive' and `Stone Cold Crazy'. The after-show lig (party!) at the Holiday Inn in Swiss Cottage was a memorable event.

Just before setting off to Europe to be confronted by similarly ecstatic crowds, Mel Bush gave Queen a gold plaque for selling out the entire tour.

Kicking off in Gothenburg, Sweden, the band trailblazed their way throughout Scandinavia, Germany, Belgium, Holland and Barcelona, cancelling only two gigs in Scandinavia when their equipment truck was involved in an accident. But this was a minor hiccup in a story that was becoming more than just a fairytale. The reaction was the same everywhere: unrestrained enthusiasm for Queen, the band of 1974.

What a year! It was almost as if Brian's illnesses had been timed to perfection, for without that six-month recess, the `Sheer Heart Attack' album may not have been released until the following year. And when they returned with both an album and a tour, even the press seemed pleased to see them. Remarkable.

But now it was time for the band to take a short holiday away from each other, and they each retreated to their family hideaways for Christmas - and a taste of normality. Well, almost. It was difficult to entirely escape from their heady music careers as long as there was a radio or TV in the vicinity and, sure enough, Christmas Day television included a special broadcast of Granada TV's `45' featuring, of course, Queen! Brian, at home with his parents in Feltham, Freddie with both family and girlfriend Mary Austin, Roger with his family and John with fiancée Veronica Tetzlaff - all watched in silent amazement at this appraisal of their career. It was the first time they'd really had a chance to view themselves objectively.

Successful as they'd become, the band still had a lot of work to do to maintain their profile. The fickleness of the music business demands consistency. Dynamic as their output in 1974 had been, the hardest part was yet to come, that is: following the ultimate high of `Sheer Heart Attack' and `Killer Queen'. It could be difficult. But then again, Queen were full of surprises...

CHAPTER TEN

A KIND OF MAGIC
1975-1976

"...It was tongue-in-cheek and it was mock opera. A lot of people slammed `Bohemian Rhapsody', but who or what can you compare it to?"
(Freddie Mercury)

Aware that 1975 was going to be even harder than the previous year, the boys extended their Christmas to ensure complete rest. For Brian, a proper holiday was essential, and in January he headed out to Tenerife in the Canary Islands for a couple of weeks. Coincidentally, Tenerife was where Brian's zodiacal light apparatus had been shipped out to years ago - so perhaps he was also checking up on any observations his construction may've recorded, as well as taking a vacation. Could he *never* relax?! John Deacon, meanwhile, took advantage of the break to marry long-term girlfriend Veronica on 18th January. This event, oddly enough, would help instigate a serious row between the band and Trident before the end of the year, culminating in a complete split from the company.

Reuniting after their respective holidays, the band immediately set to work editing the Rainbow video into the thirty-three minute film `Queen At The Rainbow', to be shown throughout cinemas in the spring of 1976, supporting Burt Reynolds' `Hustle'.

Publicly, they were still keeping their heads up, as the third single off `Sheer Heart Attack', the fairly unmemorable `Now I'm Here' - written by Brian from his hospital bed - reached No 11. For the time being, they could go no further in the U.K. and Europe. It was there in black-and-white, as Music Week screamed out the headline: `QUEEN CONQUER EUROPE'. In the music papers' Readers' Poll awards, they featured heavily in all the top categories.... Second `Best Newcomer' and second `Best Single' for `Killer Queen' in Record Mirror; eighth `Best British Group', seventh `Best Stage Band', fourth `Most Promising Group In The World' and third `Most Promising Group In Britain' in the NME. And in Disc, they came top in four categories: `Top Live Group', `Top International Group', `Top British Group' and `Best Single' for `Killer Queen', whilst `Sheer Heart Attack' was voted third `Best LP' of 1974.

Both Queen and Europe needed a rest from each other - time to let their achievements of last year sink in. But they'd be back.

It was time to sort out unfinished business in the States and, biting their nails in anticipation, they headed across the Atlantic again to start their Stateside tour in Columbus, Ohio on 5th February. This time, they were playing their own headline gigs - and, bringing them firmly back down to earth, it dawned on them that they were not quite world status yet. Far from playing arena-size venues, the band were still at the small-ish end of the gig circuit, playing 3000/4000 capacity halls. However, it was obvious to the sharp-minded American businessmen at Elektra that, out of the newest crop of bands, Queen would be the ones to make it. As the tour progressed, `Sheer Heart Attack' slid up to No 20 in the Billboard Charts, `Killer Queen' No 12. But still, Elektra had to make sure the group paid their dues before giving them that red carpet treatment...

The American tour was a lengthy and rigorous one. Covering a potential thirty-seven gigs in three months, the pace began to tell on Freddie's throat by the time they reached Philadelphia on 23rd February. After playing the Erlinger Theatre there that night, Freddie was diagnosed as having laryngitis and ordered to rest for a few days. The Washington D.C. show the following night, however, had to go ahead, as it was much too short notice to cancel. But gigs in Pittsburg, Kutztown, Buffalo, Toronto, Kitchener, London and Davenport were cancelled, and the band promised to reschedule these when humanly possible. Rumours of Freddie needing laser-beam treatment were concocted by some eager journalist and immediately denounced by the band as they resumed their tour ten days later at the Mary E Sawyer Auditorium, Wisconsin on 5th March.

A month later, the same problem reared its ugly head again, and the band began to seriously wonder if sickness was to be the bane of their entire career. The last Stateside gig, in Portland, Oregon on 7th April, was cancelled and the exhausted band left for a ten-day holiday in Hawaii on 8th April so that Freddie could rest his voice. Once again, the forced period of incarceration gave them a chance to reflect on the state of play in the U.S. Brian recalls the first time they played Los Angeles (at the Civic Auditorium, Santa Monica on 29th March):

"I remember going to Los Angeles the first

time, we sold out a couple of nights in a small place, and I went to see Led Zeppelin at the Forum. And I thought `Jesus Christ, if we can ever play here, that would be the ultimate dream come true!'"

And, of course, they would play there one day. In the meantime, there were other parts of the world to conquer - though, when Queen arrived in Japan, it was evident that they already *had* conquered that particular part of the world. Arriving at Tokyo Airport on 18th April, they were stunned to see a crowd of 3000 screaming fans waiting for them to step onto the tarmac. Dave Thomas, who was by now co-managing the band with Jack Nelson, remembers:

"They were absolutely amazed - and somewhat overwhelmed. When they went down the steps, there was a large limousine waiting to drive them to their hotel, where there were more crowds of people milling around in the foyer and in the grounds outside...and they discovered to their astonishment that each member of the group had been allocated a bodyguard because it was thought there was a real risk that they might be injured if they left their hotel bedrooms."

By an odd quirk of fate, Japan had acknowledged Queen as a world status band before any other country. During their short tour of the country, both `Sheer Heart Attack' and `Killer Queen' travelled smoothly up their respective charts till they could go no further. Elektra in Japan were certainly doing their jobs. The band were treated like kings, selling out 10,000-seater venues everywhere, including two nights at the legendary Budokan (the Martial Arts Hall in Tokyo), at the beginning and end of the tour. Hysteria reigned - girls were being dragged unconscious from packed auditoriums, the band hustled from stage to limousine to avoid being torn limb-from-limb by screaming fans, and gifts were being thrown at them from all quarters. Brian, who'd been playing his Dad's treasured war-time ukulele all this time, almost burst into tears when presented with a special Japanese `uke' - a toy koto - by one fan.

It was almost ridiculous, like a parody of Beatlemania. Even the Japanese press were going totally overboard about the band, contrary to the cynical British media. But there was nothing suspect about the astonishing Japanese reaction, it was just the way they were. Queen were deeply touched by the overwhelming respect they were greeted with. Before setting foot in Japan, Freddie had casually declared:

"I am looking forward to going...all those geisha boys and girls!"

But afterwards, still reeling from the exhilaration of it all, he revealed to Melody Maker:

"It started the moment we got there, riots at the airport, bodyguards, just like the old Beatle days. The organisation was spellbinding, and we loved every minute of it. Yes, we needed protection. You couldn't go down into the lobby of the hotel, it would be infested...but they were really nice people, waiting for autographs. And I couldn't believe the crowds at the concerts, all milling about, swaying and singing."

As well as the "geisha boys and girls", Freddie was also impressed by the beautiful and dignified culture of Japan. Grabbing as much objets d'art as he could take through customs, he vowed to return to the country as soon as possible to continue building up his Japanese art collection. It was to be a hobby Freddie would indulge in for the rest of his life.

Returning to England in May was like being dropped from a great height. From five-star hotels in Japan to their own humble abodes in London, the culture-shock took a while to get used to. But this, after all, was reality - something they would need more and more as they progressed step-by-step up the ladder. Freddie retreated to the open arms of Mary Austin in their Holland Park flat; Brian to his rented flat in Kensington; John to his wife Veronica and their house in Fulham; and Roger to his flat in Kew where he'd lived since the days of the first album.

The boys couldn't afford to move from the homes they'd held for the past three years. They were still only earning a paltry £50 per week allowance because, claimed Trident, the expense of sending Queen off round the world was enormous. Perhaps the band's suspicions over the amount they were earning was unjustified in such circumstances. Or perhaps Trident were holding back. Whatever, the money situation was causing a rift between the two parties. But, for the moment, the object of contention could wait - the band had another album to plan, and needed no distractions.

`A Night At The Opera' - the title taken from the Marx Brothers' movie - proved to be Queen's most ambitious project yet. Taking two months to rehearse, and three months to record in a total of six different studios, the album was to take the band into the seriously unbeatable league. It was pompous, bombastic, covered a staggering pastiche of styles, and was incredibly painstaking to work on. The band's concern about improving on `Sheer Heart Attack' was almost obsessive. The fourth album couldn't just be `better' than the third, it had to exceed it on every level: production, presentation, creativity, musicianship. Many people accused the band of being paranoid, but their repartee to that was merely:

"It isn't paranoia, we just want to get it right."

Spending the whole of June and July sketching out the twelve songs, the band moved into Rockfield Studios in August to lay down Roger's drum-tracks. (Rockfield is famous for its excellent drum sound and its associations with Dave Edmunds.) Multi-track vocals (of which there were many) were recorded at the Roundhouse and Brian's multiple guitar layers at Sarm. But there was more. The band sought out the particular specialities of Olympic, Scorpio and Landsdowne Studios to finely tune their epic creation. And, through it all, the eternally patient Roy Thomas Baker handled the tensions, the dissatisfaction, the irrationalities of four wired-up musical temperaments. He knew it would be worth it in the long run.

The rows during those sessions were some of the worst the band had experienced. Tension and anxiety were rife, they had to create perfection here! Each musician was getting so wrapped up in his own contribution that there were great chasms of time when they hardly saw each other at all! Brian: "The relationship got very strained sometimes. I got very worried once that I was going out on a limb and that the rest of the band didn't really approve of what I was doing. It

happened on a track off `A Night At The Opera` -
`Good Company`. I spent days and days doing
these trumpets and trombones and trying to get
into the character of those instruments. The others
were doing other things and they'd pop in from
time to time and say: `Well, you haven't done
much since we last saw you...'!"

Meanwhile, in September, the band's
long-running dispute with Trident
and Jack Nelson finally came to a
head. Queen's obvious hatred for manager Nelson
allegedly manifested itself in the opening track of
`A Night At The Opera` - the hugely vitriolic
`Death On Two Legs (Dedicated To...)`. To this
day, Queen deny the rumour that they had to fork
out £50,000 to a certain `aggrieved party` to
prevent injunctions against the issue of `a certain
track on the album'. The reasons for the band's
loathing of Nelson are still shady, possibly
because there were so many...

According to some sources, the real problems
started on the U.S. tour earlier in the year. Jack
Nelson travelled everywhere with the band, and it
may have just been a matter of bad chemistry
between Queen, particularly Freddie, and
manager. Throughout that tour, the group had
beenapproached by budding Queen managers
who'd claimed they could take them to greater
heights than anyone else - and pay them more.
That may've peeved Nelson somewhat. In fact, he
had his own row brewing with Trident at the
same time, and parted company with them in July,
subsequently moving back to the States. At the
time, the company admitted to a certain relief that
they no longer had management control over
Queen, as they'd felt uncomfortable with the
arrangement from the start. They hoped that with

Jack Nelson now out of the picture, the band would agree to still allow production and publishing responsibilities to be handled by Trident. But this was not to be the case. The band wanted *out* of any obligation to the company.

It all came down to money. Sure, Trident were pouring thousands of pounds into the band - to date £190,000 - but surely they were worth more than £50 per week each? They were, by now, very hot property indeed, and they did not think their salaries reflected their status.

Trident claimed that, unlike requirements in most management contracts, they never deducted commission from record royalties, although they did accept production points. That, in fact, is probably where the main problem between Trident and Nelson lay: Jack Nelson may not have liked the idea that Trident weren't gleaning any management royalties from the band for his own pocket, and that would've been ample reason for him to leave. But still, Queen themselves would've countered with the following argument: if they weren't giving Trident any management points, where was the extra money going? Putting Nelson out of the picture was not, for them, the answer - although it was a start!

The final straw came when John Deacon asked for an advance of £4000 so that he and his pregnant wife could set up home. The response was an outright `No!'. So, in September 1975, Queen officially split with Trident. It could've been difficult. Trident could've completely frozen all Queen activity, but instead they plumped for a severance fee (to be paid over a set period of time) and a certain percentage of the band's next six albums. In addition, the company also retained their rights to all Queen's product to date, including the `Queen At The Rainbow' film. It was a fair deal. It would not have been in Trident's interests to freeze Queen's ability to create more assets.

Unfortunately, casting themselves adrift from Trident also meant losing publicist Tony Brainsby, whom Queen valued highly. As a sign of respect, each member of the band phoned Tony privately at home to say how sorry they were about the split, and to thank him for his work.

Meanwhile, Freddie, in an interview with the NME, expressed his feelings for Trident in no uncertain terms: "As far as Queen are concerned our old management is deceased. They cease to exist in any capacity with us whatsoever. One leaves them behind like one leaves excreta. We feel so relieved!"

More privately, a dejected Freddie was heard to remark: "Trust has become a very funny word... You learn to keep your defences up."

Queen signed their own deals with EMI and Elektra - and gratefully handed over the reins of management to the highly-respected John Reid, who was working with Elton John, amongst others. Reid was not one of the managers who'd been badgering them in the States - the band themselves had approached him through `intermediary' David Croker, EMI Records' label manager.

By now, the album - a complete work of art evidently - was almost near completion. It hadn't been an entirely solid three months' work though: apart from clearing away the dead wood, Brian had nipped off for a day to act as a judge at the annual Melody Maker National Folk/Rock competition; and he and Freddie, during their sessions at Sarm, had taken time out to produce and contribute, respectively, guitar, piano and vocals to a project by solo vocalist Eddie Howell. The resultant single, `Man From Manhattan' was released in September on WEA. They also helped out a soul outfit called Trax, but no product has ever been discovered from this particular session.

The recording sessions for `A Night At The Opera' had, indeed, been rigorous, and the release date seemed to be evading the press. It was almost as if the band were reluctant to let anyone hear the completed work. Of course, rumours of a split in the Queen camp were inevitable: everything seemed to point towards it. The split with management, cancellation of an Empire Pool gig in the summer, the band's retreat from the public eye, postponement of their autumn tour, and now the delay in the album's release. It was all just the band's perfectionism of course and, to everyone's relief, they publicly introduced their new manager and announced the release dates for a single and album at a press reception in London on 19th September 1975. At the same time, they were presented with Silver and Gold discs for `Sheer Heart Attack' and `Killer Queen', a Gold for `Queen II' and a Silver for `Queen'.

When Queen unveiled their mighty hors d'oeuvres at the end of October, everyone suddenly understood why they'd been so quiet for so long. If `Bohemian Rhapsody' was just the starter, what on earth would the whole meal - the album - be like?! An entire operatic symphony?

`Bo Rap' - as the band dubbed the single - was like nothing anyone had heard before. One baffled reviewer, obviously lost for words, described it as `one of the most peculiar singles of the year'. It was certainly the longest-ever single, a mighty five minutes and fifty-five seconds (cut from eight!), and certainly the most lavish, the most extraordinary... Freddie's gargantuan, operatic-style surrealist symphony had caused great consternation within their record company. A gamble, good grief how was anyone supposed to dance to something so...so magnificent?! The record-buying public were used to simplicity, the usual easy bump-and-grind stuff. Freddie himself had spent many a sleepless night asking himself the same question, until friend and DJ Kenny Everett intervened - and cheekily forced the single's release:

"I remember getting a call from Freddie one night. He said `Ken, I was in the studios the other day and I've finished off this new single. But it's about eight minutes long and I don't know whether it's going to be a hit.' I said `Bring it over, we'll stick it on one of my tape machines in the studio and give it a listen. I doubt if anyone will play it if it's as long as that because people are frightened of long records.' So Freddie brought it over and plonked it on the machine and, of course, this glorious operatic wonder of `Bohemian Rhapsody' came out. I said `Oh forget about it, it could be half an hour long - it's going to be No 1 for centuries.'

"He was very unsure about this piece of genius. It was very odd when you look back on it in retrospect, because it was so great. It's like Mozart saying: `I don't know whether my clarinet concerto is going to take off'. It's silly really. I mean it's got No 1 written all over it from the first note."

Freddie gave Kenny a copy of the song and made him vow solemnly not to play it to anyone. That, of course, was like leaving a bag of sweets with a small child and telling him not to eat them! The outrageous Everett naturally couldn't contain himself and on his show the following weekend, he cheekily repeated the promise he'd given Freddie to his listeners, adding `Oops, my finger's slipped!' as the opening bars to the great rock opera wafted through the airwaves... His finger slipped a total of fourteen times that weekend - sending EMI into a total panic. The following Monday the record shops were besieged with people demanding a copy of Queen's new single which, of course, hadn't yet been released due to the record company's humming and haa-ing policy. They were insensed that the band should've allowed such a `person' access to `Bohemian Rhapsody' - but Everett's (and Freddie's?) ploy had worked. The single (with Roger Taylor's `I'm In Love With My Car' on the B-side) was rush released on 31st October - and predictably shot straight in at No 1, remaining in the charts for seventeen weeks, and still at the top over Christmas.

Eventually the band would receive the highly-respected seal of approval from both the British Phonographic Industry and the British Record Industry Britannia Awards for `Bohemian Rhapsody' - awards for `Best Single of 1975' from the former, and joint `Best Pop Single Of The Last Twenty-Five Years' (tying with Procul Harum's `A Whiter Shade Of Pale') from the latter, surpassing anything that even The Beatles had released! High praise indeed...

Meanwhile, as the grand opera seeped behind the Iron Curtain, Buckingham Palace started receiving sackloads of post from Russia addressed to `Queen, London'. The fanmail was duly redirected to Queen's fan club! But there was more. Queen were beginning to affect the whole structure of the music business. The accompanying video for `Bo Rap' introduced a whole new marketing tactic: promotional videos to boost record sales! The band's idea, of course, had merely been to project and accentuate the single with a suitable backdrop when they appeared on Top Of The Pops. Little did they realise that the grand `Bohemian Rhapsody' video would start a rock'n'roll revolution.

Of course, everyone wanted to know everything about `Bohemian Rhapsody', the single and the video: how long they took to make, where the idea came from, what instruments were used, and so on and so forth.

First off, no synthesisers were used on the single (as with the album). The whole of the song was incredibly complex, but one particular section - the choral part - featured a mammoth 180 precision vocal overdubs and enough of Brian's guitar parts to drown an entire real orchestra! Roy Thomas Baker explained in more depth:

"`Bohemian Rhapsody' wasn't all recorded in one go. We did the whole of the first section and the rock section, and for the middle part, we just hit some drums now and then, after which it was basically edits - we just lengthened the middle section depending on what vocals were put in, because Freddie would come up with amazing ideas. He'd walk in and say `I've got some new ideas for the vocals - we'll stick some Galileos in here...'. I'd say that that track, on its own, took getting on for three weeks. People were getting value for money - they were able to buy a single which was seven minutes long (not quite), and was three weeks work on the A-side alone! Just the basic backing track was done over a two-day period..."

Freddie obliged with the following repartee to any controversy about the song's origins:

"'Bohemian Rhapsody' didn't just come out of thin air. I did a bit of research, although it was tongue-in-cheek and it was mock opera. Why not? I certainly wasn't saying I was an opera fanatic and I knew everything about it. A lot of people have slammed 'Bohemian Rhapsody', but who can you compare it to? Name one group that's done an operatic single. We were adamant that the track could be a hit in its entirety."

The video - filmed on 10th November - cost a paltry (by today's standards) £4500 to make and only took four hours to film, as there was a rush to provide something for Queen's Top Of The Pops appearance the following week! Directed by Bruce Gowers, the video encapsulated the atmosphere of the single - a dark, gothic commentary of a man's tragic life in full colour. The band, in the choral 'Galileo' break, were featured in similar pose to that on the cover of 'Queen II', the four in head-and-shoulders posture looking upwards into a beam of light. It was to become their most famous pose. John:

"People used to have clips before, but they were often shot on film. It was quite accidental...at the time we were about to tour England, and we knew we wouldn't be able to get to record 'Top Of

The Pops' on the Wednesday. Our managers at the time had a mobile unit, so it was actually shot on video, in only a few hours!"

In the meantime, `A Night At The Opera' had been aired at an exclusive reception at the Roundhouse on 7th November. Its release date was set for 3rd December. Costing around £30,000/£40,000 to make, the album was worth its weight in gold, a spectacular, diverse platter of unpredictable foibles (care of Freddie), experimental musical strands (care of Brian). It was every bit as grandiose and flamboyant as they'd claimed it would be - and still no synthesisers! Freddie's birthsign logo, reflecting the band's status, had been vamped up and enlarged to hog almost the entire album sleeve.

On 14th November 1975, Queen finally started their much-anticipated British tour, now an annual feature of their schedule. Supported by Mr Big, they burned round the major venue circuit, kicking up a storm wherever they went. Opening with two riotous nights at Liverpool Empire, and playing a total of five nights at the Hammersmith Odeon, the tour proved once and for all that Queen had become one of Britain's established acts.

After the fourth consecutive Hammersmith gig, halfway through the tour, `A Night At The Opera' was released. Its immediate escalation to No 1 confirmed the band's position - there was simply no stopping such a glorious talent. Hogging both album and singles charts, the band themselves were ecstatic, over the moon - but perhaps wondering how much higher they could go?

As a mark of the tour's success, the band took

in an extra, fifth night at Hammersmith on Christmas Eve, filmed live for a special edition of `The Old Grey Whistle Test', and simultaneously broadcast on Radio One. That night, Brian's and Freddie's parents met for the first time - despite being neighbours for almost sixteen years!

The Bulsaras presence at that gig was, perhaps, a small breakthrough for Freddie's relationship with his stoically traditional parents. But still, throughout his career, it was obvious they never entirely approved of his outrageously camp stage presence that questioned their son's sexuality. It began to dawn on everyone around him that he'd never once denied any `gay' accusations, and perhaps the image he so enjoyed flaunting was, in fact, a reflection of his own private desires? Through Queen, maybe Freddie was beginning to discover aspects of his character that he may not have acknowledged before.

His stage presence was overwhelmingly flamboyant - dear Freddie did love to dress up! As if acting out some obscene cabaret, he'd change in and out of a selection of lavish, daring outfits throughout Queen's set, sometimes appearing in full drag, sometimes in painfully-tight sequinned catsuits - adapting his image like a chameleon to the band's ever-changing moods. Freddie was, in a sense, Queen's canvas - the visual projection of their music.

But sadly, much as everyone assumed Freddie was a natural extrovert - how could he not be? - he was, in fact, a typical introvert. Blinding people with his image of exaggerated gestures, he successfully smothered his insecurities, letting no-one in on his personal secrets. As he once said:

"People are apprehensive when they meet me. They think I'm going to eat them. But underneath it all I'm quite shy."

He was, in fact, the ultimate professional - his job was to entertain people, not to burden them with his personal problems. Brian made the observation at the time that he hardly knew Freddie at all, even though he'd been with him for five years now. And Freddie himself pointed out: "I want my privacy and I feel I've given a lot for it."

Freddie - as the rest of the band - had learnt the meaning of trust in the past year. The more established Queen became, the more everyone wanted a piece of their action. During 1975 they'd discovered the cut-throat side of the business. Experiencing cynicism for the first time had nearly split the band up, as Freddie explained: "At one point, two or three years after we began, we nearly disbanded. We felt it wasn't working, there were too many sharks in the business and it was all getting too much for us. But something inside us kept us going and we learned from our experiences, good and bad...

"When you have success it becomes really difficult because then you really learn the things behind the business. You find out the real baddies. It's like playing rock'n'roll dodgems. You've got to make sure you don't get hit too often."

Queen had learnt their most important lesson in the past year. Many bands break up when they discover the hard nose of the business, drowning in cynicism, throwing their hands in the air and begging the question: `What's the point?'. But Queen knew that their music was the point, and that if it took dealing with the "sharks in the business" to get their music to the masses, then so be it.

1976 began for Queen on 14th January with John Reid's announcement that `Bohemian Rhapsody' had already sold one million copies in Britain alone, and Freddie was accordingly awarded his second Ivor Novello award. It was a fitting way for Queen to leave their home country - for it was time, once again, to take `their music to the masses'. Queen would be away from Britain for the first third of the year, touring the States, Japan and Australia. Their profile, of course, would still retain a presence back home - all four albums kept each other company in the Top Twenty for a while - but, in effect, this year was to be relatively quiet for Queen's British fans.

Their progress through the States - which began in Connecticut on 27th January - was rock steady, although radio reluctance had, at first, stalled promotion of `A Night At The Opera' and `Bohemian Rhapsody'. However, after America's traditional rock DJs saw the wisdom of airing the single, and tracks off the album, both skidded their way up to No 3 in their respective charts. They were finally breaking through to the yanks. Confirmation of that came in New York during their four-day residency at the Beacon Theater in February, when Freddie was nearly strangled to death by a clutch of possessed female fans! Ian Hunter of Mott The Hoople happened to be in the States around the time of those gigs and, nipping backstage one night, asked the band if they'd like to help out on his solo album, `All American Alien Boy'. Freddie, Brian and Roger duly harmonised on one track, `You Nearly Done Me In', and Hunter's album was released in March.

Another hysterical tour of Japan followed, before the band flew down-under for their first full-length Aussie tour in April. There, they discovered just how far afield their music was travelling. To their surprise, they'd been booked to play a string of arena and stadium gigs in Perth, Adelaide, Sydney, Melbourne and Brisbane: all the major antipodean cities.

After touring for nearly six months, the band returned to England at the end of April, just as the `Queen At The Rainbow' film started doing the rounds of the cinema circuit with `Hustle'. After rehearsing new songs for a couple of months, the boys decided they were ready to start recording the follow-up to `A Night At The Opera'. This time, they felt they had enough studio experience to produce the album themselves. So, amicably parting company with Roy Thomas Baker in July, they trundled into Sarm and, later, Wessex Studios, leaving their June-released single, the Deacon-penned `You're My Best Friend' (No 7), to keep Queen in the public eye. This was the first single not to be released as a taster for an anticipated album.

There was nothing sinister about their split with Baker. Although he'd been a part of the Trident network, Queen had always regarded him as their friend and producer, not a corporate droid. No - Baker had taught them well, and was aware that one day they'd need to `spread their wings' in the studio, so his departure came as no surprise to anyone. Besides which, this was more a temporary parting than anything else. Baker would be back.

By September, nearly finished with the new album, the band were in dire need of a break.

Breathing in some welcome fresh air on 1st and 2nd of the month, they joined Elton John, Billy Connolly, John Miles and Rainbow at the `Festival Of Popular Music', a gala to celebrate the re-opening of the Edinburgh Playhouse. On 10th, they struck out proudly with their own open-air festival at Cardiff Castle. Entitled `Queen At The Castle', the band headlined over Manfred Mann, Andy Fairweather-Low and Frankie Miller. But the best, and most memorable was yet to come.

Only the Stones had succeeded in pulling it off before. Their free festival in Hyde Park in July 1969 had been an unprecedented victory. Only a handful of bands could hope to follow the Stones' success that day - and attract enough people to make the park a worthwhile rock festival site. Queen was one of them.

For Freddie, 18th September had been a day of solemnity and mourning since 1972. Jimi Hendrix' death had left a lasting impression on the immigrant singer, and Freddie never forgot an anniversary. This year, he and the band decided to remember Hendrix in style - by taking over Hyde Park, and Capital Radio's airwaves, for the day.

150,000 people turned up that late summer day, enjoying the rock'n'roll weirdness of Steve Hillage, or the rock and pop of Kiki Dee and Supercharge - but waiting, ultimately, for Queen. A glorious, unsurpassable event in the band's diary. They had never confronted such a massive audience before. Brian summed up their feelings of Hyde Park 1976:

"The Hyde Park gig was really high. The occasion rather than the gig, you know, the tradition of Hyde Park. I went to see the first one with the Floyd and Jethro Tull - a great atmosphere and the feeling that it was free. We felt that it would be nice to revive that but it was fraught with heartache because there were so many problems. Trying to get the place was hard enough, let alone in the evening. We had to make compromises and in the end, because the schedule overran by half-an-hour, the loss meant we couldn't do an encore.

"But I think it was one of the most significant gigs in our career. There was great affection because we'd kind of made it in a lot of other countries by that time, but England was still, you know, we weren't sure if we were really acceptable here. So it was a wonderful feeling to come back and see that crowd and get that response."

The live buzz kept the creative juices going till the final mixes of `A Day At The Races' at the end of September. Out and about in October, the band visited Kempton Park Races on 16th as a promotional tactic for the album and impending single, `Somebody To Love' (which reached No 2). The group, at John Reid's instigation, had sponsored one of the races, so the grand advertising hoardings for the forthcoming album were cunningly appropriate. Not that `A Day At The Races' needed much pushing - it turned silver even before its release date on 10th December, selling half a million in advance orders. When it got to No 1 by January 1977 (their second consecutive chart-topping album), nobody was surprised, and it certainly grabbed the attention of an American gentleman by the name of Hugh Z Hackenbush. Groucho Marx, as he was better known, sent a telegram to Queen congratulating them on the album's success, and thanking them for pinching two Marx Brothers' movie titles! The band subsequently sent him a `Queen II' tour jacket - just before the infamous actor's death.

By the end of 1976, Queen were riding higher than ever, and even the U.K. press were finally beginning to acknowledge the band's influence on British rock, ranking them alongside the likes of Genesis and Led Zeppelin.

The group were certainly leaving their mark on the unlikeliest of people - indirectly, they were responsible for presenter Bill Grundy's ousting from the `Today' programme.... They were due to appear on his show on 1st December, but had to pull out at the last minute. EMI decided to use the opportunity to expose their latest, controversial, signing - The Sex Pistols - on Grundy's chatshow. The experience was to prove terminal for Grundy, confronted on live television by the abusive punk pioneers effing and blinding their way through the interview. Shortly afterwards, the Pistols were ousted from EMI. Coincidentally, the catalogue number for the Pistols' `Anarchy In The U.K.' single - EMI 2566 - happened to be the next in sequence after Queen's `Somebody To Love'. The punk revolution may've arrived, but Queen far exceeded the Pistols in the charts at this particular juncture.

Another successful year, 1976 was probably best remembered for the record-breaking Hyde Park concert in September. The band were currently on some sort of `career plateau' - during the past year they'd merely confirmed the success of 1975 by releasing another No 1 album, pretty much presented in the same grand, regal style as `A Night At The Opera'. From hereon, with hot new bands pursuing them up the charts, the punk movement in particular pouring scorn on Queen's elegant, camp persona, the band would have to pull out the stops to maintain their appeal. Maybe a change in direction was forthcoming. Leaving Britain with a much-demanded repeat of their 1975 `Old Grey Whistle Test' performance on 28th December, the band decided to give the U.K. a complete rest for a few months. Let their native country get the punk experience out of their systems before returning. Unfortunately, their absence wouldn't be long enough. By the time they returned, they'd be landing slap bang in the middle of all that vomit...

CHAPTER ELEVEN

IN THE LAP OF THE GODS
1977-1980

*"The term rock'n'roll is just a label one starts off
with. I should like to think of it as a vast open door...."*
(Freddie Mercury)

When 1977 arrived, so did the punk movement. In the wake of that great anarchist hype, The Sex Pistols, a whole spitting, snarling revolution began. Such ugly anti-social behaviour was in direct contrast to Queen's sophisticated attitude and, though the band obviously maintained their balance, the violence of these new bands would ultimately affect their musical direction.

So leaving England to their own devices was probably the best move the band could've made. Rather than stewing in a predicted cavalcade of criticism - Queen vs The Sex Pistols - and ultimately being branded 'has beens', the band concentrated on countries where total respect was guaranteed. Unfortunately, they were underestimating the lasting power of punk...

1977 was also The Queen's Jubilee Year and, in a brilliantly-conceived marketing plot, the band were paired with Thin Lizzy for a forty-two date American tour, beginning in Wisconsin on 13th January, after a week's rehearsals in Boston. The tour's title? The 'Queen Lizzy Tour' of course! Freddie, in particular, wholly approved of celebrating The Queen's 25th anniversary: "The Jubilee's quite fun isn't it? I love The Queen. I'm very patriotic. I love all this pomp, of course I do. I love it. She does outrageous things!"

For Queen, this particular tour was one of their greatest challenges yet. A tougher, hard rock market had opened up to meet the needs of those who couldn't relate to the safety-pin brigade. Bands like UFO, The Scorpions and Thin Lizzy were gradually paving the way for the next generation of rockers - The New Wave Of British Heavy Metal. Bands like the embryonic Iron Maiden, Def Leppard and Saxon were toughening up the basic rock attitude, bringing hard rock up-to-date and calling it 'heavy metal'.

Although America hadn't quite cottoned onto what was predominantly a British conception (born on the streets of working-class England), they needed an outlet for their aggression as much as England did.

Thus Lizzy - one of the forefathers to the NWOBHM - were really more relevant to the current state of people's minds than Queen. The public wanted reality, they were beginning to shy away from what some snide journalist called 'synthetic posturing'.

When Lizzy hit the stage, it was like a kick in the balls to Queen's audience. This was rock'n'roll! Brian expressed the band's willingness to rise to the challenge: "Thin Lizzy as a support band is a real challenge. They'll want to blow us off-stage, and that can be a very healthy thing. You feed off the energy of others and I know that if they go down a real storm, then we're gonna go on feeling that much higher. It makes for good

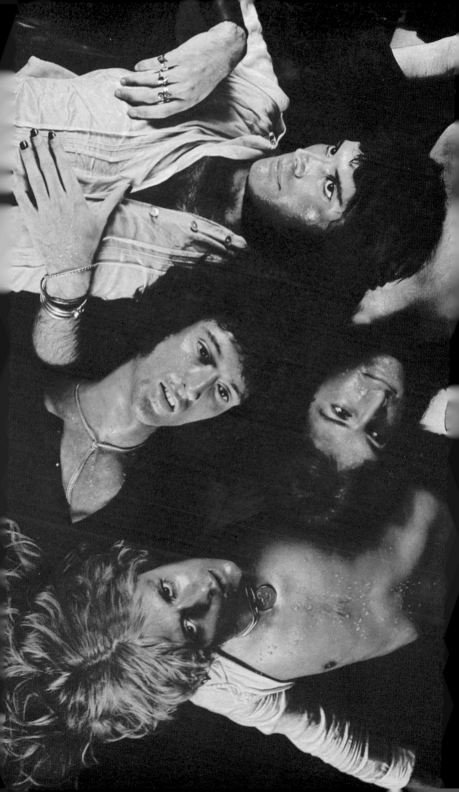

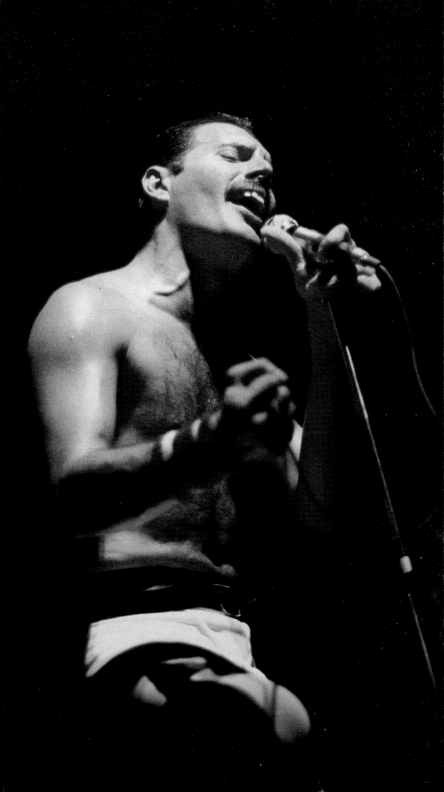

concerts. We've had it the other way round. I think we gave Mott The Hoople a hard time on our first tours of Britain and America."

Queen were aware of their need to adapt and prove that their music wasn't totally reliant on mass overdubs and production pizzazz. During that U.S. tour, they deliberately included live versions of some of the more production-inspired numbers off 'A Day At The Races': 'Millionaire Waltz', 'Somebody To Love', 'You Take My Breath Away'. Their more cynical fans appreciated the gesture - and proved to them that Queen were, after all, very much a live band.

Unfortunately, the American press weren't so convinced. Catching on to the British media's poisonous campaign against the band, they deliberately set out to antagonise the band, over-praising Lizzy, thus attempting to set the two up against each other. Their plan, of course, backfired - fêting Lizzy only brought more people to the shows! By now, Queen were used to the media's barbed comments but, as Brian revealed at the time, they weren't totally immune: "The local press have been almost unanimously anti-us. But it is very unpredictable. I don't know if they know anything about music. It certainly doesn't sound like it.... Yes, I'm affected by criticism. I think most artists are, even if they say they're not. It doesn't matter how far you get, if someone says you're a load of shit, it hurts."

As the Jubilee package tour flounced its way round America's stadiums (including the L.A. Forum, thus fulfilling Brian's ultimate dream!), the press back home were having a fine old hoot over Queen's latest single. 'Tie Your Mother Down' (from 'A Day At The Races'), released on 4th

March, failed to make it any further than 31 in the charts. More ammunition for the press! Tongues sharpened by this euphoric news, the music media lashed out at the single, the band and their apparent 'irrelevance' to the country's current state of mind. Radical young journalists were starting to champion the cause of the fashionable pseudo-anarchists. Dole queue musicians supposedly suffering the filth and grime of low-grade life were in. The odd scar or tattoo would add to the 'authenticity' of a genuine 'ardnut punk, and tales of impoverished childhood were definitely de rigueur.

Apparently, none of Queen had experienced any real pain. Their 'disgusting' displays of 'capitalist behaviour' - Freddie's penchant for toasting his audiences with champagne didn't go down too well - were regarded as tasteless and out-of-date. And when Freddie boasted: "People want art, they want showbiz. They want to see you rush off in your limousine...", you could hear music journalists gagging all the way to Zanzibar! But there was more. In one of Freddie's last interviews, the NME's Tony Stewart laid into the singer with such vehemence, it's a wonder Freddie didn't scratch his eyes out! They found no common territory whatsoever during the interview, and the resultant feature boasted the title: 'Is This Man A Prat?'. That was it for Freddie. No more interviews. Roger spoke on Freddie's behalf a little while later to explain why the singer didn't want to get involved with the press anymore:

"Freddie doesn't talk anymore because he's a little tired of Queen and himself being misrepresented. I think anybody who meets Freddie would be in for a bit of a surprise. He's not quite the prima donna you might imagine. Obviously, he's a positive character, but so are we all. When all is said and done, he works damned hard and puts on a good show."

In all truth, Freddie was starting to over-indulge in the glamorous life-style, and his reputation for excess in all areas was spreading fast. Whilst the rest of the band were comparatively monogamous - John had dragged Veronica and baby round the American circuit and Brian was now married as well - Freddie seemed to be involved in some sort of sexual competition with himself. He hated to be alone for a moment and, as such, made sure he always had 'company' at night. But none of his liaisons ever came to anything. At the time, he was often heard to boast: "I'm a good lay. I'll go to bed with anything. My sex drive is enormous. I live life to the full."

But in later years, a wiser Freddie would look back in regret: "I've had a lot of lovers, I've tried relationships on either side - male and female, but all of them went wrong. Love is like Russian roulette for me. I try to hold back when I'm attracted to someone but I just can't control love. It runs riot. All my one-night stands are just me playing a part."

Freddie's drinking habits were also getting worse. He could, apparently, down a whole bottle of vodka - his favourite tipple - in one go. And there were the parties too: never-ending, outrageous sessions that would've shocked even the hardiest of party-animals. One particular birthday party of Freddie's was held aboard Concorde, each guest being sent a first-class ticket to New York. The party boogied on for days, the guests drinking their way through £50,000-worth of champagne - never mind the other expenses.

As a result of Freddie's lust for sex and alcohol, he and Mary Austin split after seven years of living together. He was becoming too sexually loose to continue a normal relationship. Mary:

"I would have married him if he'd been heterosexual. I was devastated when we stopped living together, but strangely enough, our closeness just grew over the years."

Indeed, the two kept on loving each other right to the end - they really were the ultimate soul partnership. In 1979, they did attempt to reunite, but Freddie's bisexuality had become too integrated by then. When Mary suggested to him that they have a child together, his retort was somewhat discouraging. He replied: "I'd rather have another cat."

But the following admission from Freddie in later years revealed the depth of his feelings towards Mary, and how large a part she continued to play in his life:

"Our love affair ended in tears, but a deep bond grew out of it, and that's something nobody can take away from us. It's unreachable. All my lovers ask me why they can't replace her, but it's simply impossible. I don't feel jealous of her lovers because, of course, she has a life to lead, and so do I. Basically, I try to make sure she's happy with whoever she's with, and she tries to do the same for me. We look after each other, and that's a wonderful form of love. I might have all the problems in the world, but I have Mary and that gets me through."

When they first broke up in 1977, Freddie bought Mary a £400,000 four-bedroomed house in Kensington, only a couple of blocks from his own, recently-acquired (in cash!) twenty-eight room £500,000 'Garden Lodge' at 1 Logan Place, Kensington, with its high walls and secret garden. But, though they lived so close to each other, Freddie might as well have been on Mars, he was away so much - indeed, it took him more than four years to actually settle into the house!:

"Every person who makes a lot of money has a dream he wants to carry out, and I achieved that dream with this wonderful house. Whenever I watched Hollywood movies set in plush homes with lavish decor, I wanted that for myself, and now I've got it. But to me it was much more important to get the damn thing than to actually go and live in it. Maybe the challenge has worn off now. I'm very much like that - once I get something, I'm not that keen on it anymore. I still love the house, but the real enjoyment is that I've achieved it.

"Sometimes, when I'm alone at night, I imagine that when I'm fifty I'll creep into that house as my refuge, and then I'll start making it a home. Anyways, as it is, I can only spend sixty days a year in England for tax reasons."

Freddie's excessive nature, of course, reflected in his extravagant stage presence (or vice versa). The ultimate high for him was to take his audience on journeys they'd never forget - to pull out all stops for the pleasure of their entertainment. With the emergence of a savage new breed of musicians intent on beating the aggression out of their audiences, Queen became even more determined to charm their own fans with elegance and pizzazz. The Jubilee tour was certainly their most extraordinary in terms of visual splendour. Freddie:

"I like people to go away from a Queen show feeling fully entertained, having had a good time. I think Queen songs are pure escapism, like going to see a good film - after that, they can go away and say that was great, and go back to their problems.

"I don't want to change the world with our music. There are no hidden messages in our songs, except for some of Brian's. I like to write songs for fun, for modern consumption. People can discard them like a used tissue afterwards. You listen to it, like it, discard it, then on to the next. Disposable pop, yes."

After a brief stint in Europe, the band returned to England at the end of May to continue celebrating the Jubilee year at home. Bravely ignoring the media's spittle showers, they strode purposefully round Britain's major gig circuit, culminating the tour with two massive, budget-busting shows at Earls Court on 6th and 7th June 1977. At these gigs, Queen unveiled their piéce de resistance - a 26ft high, 54ft wide, 5000lb, £50,000 'Crown'-shaped lighting rig. The elaborate metal construction rose up majestically at the beginning of each gig to reveal the four musicians. The band themselves were decked out in their most dazzling costumes yet.

The press hated Queen for this 'obscene' display of wealth, and did their best to convince the public that they should hate the band too. One thing they did forget to mention, of course, was that Queen had lost £75,000 putting on the Earls

Court gigs, and that all proceeds had gone to The Queen's Jubilee charity fund.

To coincide with the British tour, Queen's first EP was released, featuring 'Good Old Fashioned Loverboy', 'Death On Two Legs', 'Tenement Funster' and 'White Queen'. Virgin Records, now handling The Sex Pistols, ensured that the two bands stayed in the ring together by releasing the Pistols' irreverent version of 'God Save The Queen' at the same time. Both EP and single entered the charts on 4th June but, alas, the Pistols were to win this particular round, pogoing their way to No 2, leaving Queen behind at 17.

But, however much the press attempted to upset the band by championing the Pistols and their kin to the hilt, Queen refused to rise to the bait. Just to throw a spanner into the media's works, it turned out that the group had nothing against the punk movement. Much to the music press' dismay, Brian was quoted as saying:

"I'll say one thing for punk rock at the moment. It is creating a way for groups which I think is maybe very healthy...."

He was hinting that Queen were about to change direction. That, far from being beaten into submission by the punk crusaders, they were actually fascinated by this new musical trend. Sucking in their modern environment and studying its curious little foibles, they were about to prove that anything anyone else could do - they could do better! Everyone was in for a big surprise within the next few months...

However, whilst the band were busy self-producing their sixth album at Basing Street and

Wessex Studios between June and October, the music press found another piece of ammunition. When Roger Taylor's solo single, 'I Wanna Testify', appeared in August 1977, it was apparently proof positive that Queen were about to split up. According to them, Roger could no longer tolerate being the band's third songwriter, and was branching out on his own. Not only that but, said the press, the relationship between Mercury and May - which, it was true, had always been that of 'close colleagues' rather than friends - was almost at breaking point. All this was total fabrication of course.

When Roger's single flopped, the attitude of Queen's fans was a relieved 'serves him right'. But he wasn't the only one to dabble in other projects. Later in the year, Brian - along with Ringo Starr, Elton John, Ron Wood and Leo Sayer - would contribute to Lonnie Donegan's 'come-back' album 'Putting On The Style', playing guitar on a track called 'Diggin' My Potatoes'. And Freddie and Roy Thomas Baker had already co-produced an album entitled 'This One's On Me' by Peter Straker. None of these, including Roger's single, were any big deal, but still the rumours persisted.

Rather than issue statements refuting the split, Queen remained silent for a painfully long two months. And then, on 7th October, they did issue a statement of sorts. The release of the perfectly-paired A- and B-side 'We Are The Champions'/'We Will Rock You' dumbfounded everyone. Not only did it prove that Freddie and Brian were totally in tune with each other (Freddie wrote the A-side, Brian the B-), but also that Queen were categorically catering for a wider market. Whilst the NME muttered lamely that 'We Will Rock You' was a 'near-clone of Gary Glitter's

'Rock'n'Roll Pt II', 'We Are The Champions' was rapidly becoming a favourite anthem on the football terraces in England, and at sporting events of all kinds world-wide. Reaching No 2 in the U.K. (against the Pistols' No 8 'Holidays In The Sun'), No 4 in the States, it topped the charts in Holland, Israel, South Africa and Brazil.

When the new album, 'News Of The World' (released on 28th October) followed suit by selling 7,000,000 copies world-wide (and blistering up to No 4 in the U.K.), the press found themselves drowning in champagne... Of course, they tried to forecast doom for the band who could incorporate so many popular styles in one album. Apparently, it signalled a lack of direction. But to any intelligent punter, it represented a rebirth, a broad-mindedness, a willingness and ability to adapt. As Freddie commented:

"I just like to think we've come through rock'n'roll, call it what you like, and there are no barriers; it's open. Especially now when everybody's putting their feelers out, and they want to infiltrate new territories. This is what I've been trying to do for years."

Ironically, during sessions for 'News Of The World', Queen discovered The Sex Pistols right next door recording 'Never Mind The Bollocks'. And, for the fourth time, the two bands found themselves on the record shop shelves at exactly the same time! Roger Taylor remembered a particularly amusing exchange between Freddie and Sid Vicious in the studio one day:

"One day Sid stumbled in on our recording sessions. He yelled at Freddie: 'Ullo Fred, so you've really brought ballet to the masses then!'.

Freddie just turned round and said 'Ah, Mr Ferocious. Well, we're trying our best dear!'"

In actual fact, the two bands had a great deal of respect for each other. And the Pistols' influence definitely affected Queen. Taylor's 'Sheer Heart Attack' from the album was out-and-out punk, the whole album generally harsher than their previous output.

The album sleeve alone caused a wave of intrigue. The first to be designed by somebody outside the band, it was a total departure from the regal presentation of 'A Night At The Opera' and 'A Day At The Races'. The cover featured a drawing of a robot giant holding the lifeless forms of Brian and Freddie in his hand, John and Roger falling into an open pit below. It was an adaptation of a Frank Kelly Freas cartoon that Brian and Roger had remembered from the cover of an old sci-fi comic. After tracking Freas down in Virginia, USA, they'd persuaded him to redesign his original illustration.

With the title 'News Of The World' splashed across the top of the album sleeve, it was pretty obvious that Queen were painting a picture of the media's attitude towards them. Some caught the irony, some didn't.

Returning to the States on 11th November to continue their world tour, Queen discovered that 'We Are The Champions' had already made its impact on the nation. The band were welcomed with open arms. At last, they'd broken through to the States.

In 1977, Queen had had to face that dreaded stage in a band's career when youth threatens to usurp their position. But they'd confronted hostility without batting an eyelid, persisting with their united vision, yet surrendering to the need for flexibility and change (which included Freddie, John and Roger donning new shorter haircuts!). As a result, they were as prominent as the Pistols in the music papers' Readers' Polls for 1977. They were certainly pouring scorn on that old adage: 'You can't teach an old dog new tricks'!

Queen had always been assertive, but their first move of 1978 proved just how confident they really were. In February, they decided it was time to set up their own management structure, after two-and-a-half years with John Reid. Severing their agreement with Reid in typical style - in the back of Freddie's Rolls Royce during filming for the 'We Will Rock You' video at Roger's house in Surrey - the band set up their own company, Queen Productions. Freddie's statement on the split was shady to say the least:

"We simply don't need a manager like John anymore. We're in a position to guide our own careers..."

Brian confirmed Freddie's feelings: "We didn't particularly want the job of managing ourselves, but we decided it was the best way of getting precisely what we wanted, and controlling our own destiny."

Appointing themselves directors of Queen Productions, the band would draw salaries of £690,000 each in the year 1978/79 - and eventually they'd become the highest-paid directors in British industry. A far cry from the £50 per week they were earning only three years ago... John Deacon was the man voted in as chief financier, his keen business sense finally finding an avenue. Brian describes the elusive Deacon personality:

"John dominates business in the sense of legal dealings with other people, which he's very hot on. He's the only one of us who can really keep up with what's going on.

"He doesn't let anybody off with anything. He knows more than anybody about the equipment. We have a very good crew now, but in the past John has been called on on many occasions at the last minute to fix things. He's a bass-player and has a bass-player's mentality in many ways. He's very solid and no-nonsense. He's always got his feet firmly on the ground. He's needed particularly with Freddie and me because we tend to go off at tangents without any thought of where we're coming back to. Deacy will sit there and bring us back down."

Having cleared away more dead wood, the band headed off to Scandinavia on 12th April to start their European tour. Their latest single, 'Spread Your Wings' (released in February), had not done at all well in the charts, staggering up to only 34, but Queen were by now so established, one bum single every now and then could do them little harm. The European visit was predictably successful, particularly their first gigs in Paris, at the Pavilion on 23rd and 24th April, when the seven thousand-capacity audience for each gig stood throughout the two-and-a-half hour set. "Well that's Paris ticked off.." Freddie was heard to comment on his way to the dressing-room on the last night.

By now, Queen's British fans were beginning to

feel neglected. The previous year, there had been no full-length U.K. tour and, after witnessing the magnificent Earls Court gigs, they were beginning to wonder if Britain's venues were big enough for Queen's splendid shows. By now the band had such a mass of equipment that, wherever they went, they were followed by a whole caravan of vehicles: seven tractor trailers in total, which included in its cargo a lighting rig of over four hundred separate lights weighing in at five tons. Their British fans' concern certainly had foundation. This year, it dawned on everyone how untouchable Queen were becoming. Once again, there was no British tour as such. Instead, two shows were booked at Stafford Bingley Hall on 6th and 7th May, two at the Empire Pool, Wembley, on 11th and 12th. All four were magnificently choreographed, expensively equipped - and totally sold out.

Honour upon honour was being heaped upon Queen. Most recently, they'd received the 'Best Group' award at the Daily Mail British Pop and Rock Awards ceremony. And, when EMI were presented with the Queen's Award To Industry in July, they chose to celebrate the event by pressing three hundred copies of 'Bohemian Rhapsody' on Royal Purple vinyl. Queen had passed the point where a band can be dragged down by the press or the business. They were no longer mere minstrels dependent on businessmen for favours. On the contrary, Queen were themselves an integral part of the music business empire now. Untouchable indeed. All four owned the most luxurious of homes - in July, Roger bought himself a house just outside Guildford, complete with twenty acres of land and a potent legacy as the previous home of Dr Crippen's lawyer! Then there were the second homes, the cars, the clothes.

These men were in the seriously wealthy bracket.... Yet, however comfortable they may've become, complacency was never an issue. All four of them could quite easily have retired there and then, as they'd certainly earned enough to see them through to old age. But they didn't - music was the reason they'd got together in the first place, why they were so comfortable now, their reason for living, in fact. What else could they do? As Freddie said:

"I don't know what else I'd do. I can't cook, I'm not a very good housewife. Basically, I'm just a musical prostitute my dear."

Thus, in July 1978, the band sank back into studio work, this time recalling Roy Thomas Baker to production duties. Whether they were not happy with their own work on the last two albums, or just felt they needed guidance after the varied directions of 'News Of The World', is open to conjecture.

Their strange new album, 'Jazz' (after Ry Cooder's album of the same name), was recorded in Mountain Studios in Montreux and Super Bear in Nice, France, for the first time utilising studio facilities outside Britain. As they were still in Nice when Freddie's birthday arrived, the band hired an exclusive night-club for the event. Everybody stripped off naked and frolicked in the swimming pool all night - except Freddie, who danced on the tables instead. So, there was a limit to his exhibitionism... But there was more bare flesh just around the corner.

What were the band playing at? As sharp-minded businessmen, Queen must've known that releasing a single with a picture of a naked, fat-bottomed girl on a bicycle on its sleeve would cause uproar. Of course they knew. The double A-sided 'Bicycle Race'/'Fat Bottomed Girls', from the forthcoming album, was released on 13th October, and subsequently withdrawn from record shops. Some bright person hastily drew panties over the girl's behind, and the overtly gimmicky single reached No 11, amidst a great deal of sexist finger-pointing from the press. NME thought that publishing a rear-view photo of Freddie with the caption 'Fat Bottomed Queen' was particularly hilarious.

But what was it all about? Neither 'Fat Bottomed Girls' nor 'Bicycle Race' had any connection with the theme of the album, 'Jazz', which followed on 10th November. A silhouetted string of naked cycling girls ran all the way round the album sleeve, but what did it all mean? Nothing apparently, except perhaps a hint of something Queen had never tackled before: sex. The album itself wreaked even more havoc with its free poster featuring hordes of - yes - naked cycling girls. Parents, particularly in America, were outraged when their kids came home brandishing copies of 'Jazz' with its 'disgusting' poster. The fold-out was duly replaced with an application form for the poster instead - and the album reached No 2 in the U.K. Whatever Queen were up to - it was working! But there was worse to come. On Queen's Stateside tour from October to December, the band exacerbated their sexism campaign by thrusting the 'Bicycle Race'/'Fat Bottomed Girls' gimmick in America's face too. During the 'Jazz' section of their set, Queen arranged for dozens of naked girls to bounce around the stage. Freddie himself was becoming more and more camp with every tour, favouring a nice line in little leather caps - and, this year, he arrived onstage astride the shoulders of two 'Superman' musclemen. More and more decadent.... To celebrate the album's release, the band threw a party in New Orleans (the home of jazz), inviting the four hundred guests to mingle with an exquisite selection of large-posteriored ladies, naked mud-wrestlers, dwarves, magicians, jugglers and - for the record company executives - some 'special' entertainment. It was like an orgy in hell! Of course there was more controversy, but two sold-out nights at New York's prestigious Madison Square Gardens made any outrage seem petty.

So, how had it all started? Pretty simple really. Freddie had written a song called 'Bicycle Race', Brian one called 'Fat Bottomed Girls' - from whence they came nobody knows - and the two had cunningly decided to link their songs together. A tenuous connection to say the least, but from that shaky foundation had come the idea to shoot a video to accompany the double A-sided single. Featuring fifty naked girls hurtling across Wimbledon Stadium (hotly pursued by various members of the panting paparazzi), the film - shot on 17th September - had been a hush-hush affair, for obvious reasons. Not even the band had attended this historic event, as they'd been too busily ensconced in the album, that strange hotch-potch of disco, jazz and r'n'b.

So what did the band have to say, in their defence, about their strange penchant for nude bicycle races? Proud new father Brian expressed Queen's new-found rebellious streak:

"We lost some of our audience with that. 'How could you do it? It doesn't go with your spiritual side.' But my answer is that the physical side is just as much a part of a person as the spiritual or intellectual side. It's fun. I'll make no apologies. All music skirts around sex, sometimes very directly. Ours doesn't. In our music, sex is either implied or referred to semi-jokingly, but it's always there."

The joke may have been delivered cack-handedly, the punch-line obscured by the subject matter - but naked girls are always guaranteed to sell product...

Returning to England at the end of December, Queen put the icing on their most controversial year to date by announcing, presumptuously, that they would be playing a gig on Wimbledon's Centre Court! The Lawn Tennis Association quickly dispensed with that idea.

So, where exactly were Queen headed? It seemed that, since the advent of the punk movement in 1977, the band's direction had been thrown into turmoil. Perhaps if punk hadn't forced them to stretch their tentacles out, the band might've continued along the pristine, disciplined lines of the two 'Marx Brothers' albums. But, surrounded by the passion and aggression of a vital new breed of musician, Queen had no choice but to meet the needs of a new generation. From the testing-ground of 'News Of The World' to the shock and confusion of 'Jazz', they would continue to explore new territories with their next studio album. But that would be a long time coming.

1979 was to be a comparatively run-of-the-mill

year. It was going to be difficult for Queen to surpass the achievements and controversies of recent years. Their plan for 1979 was simple: to tread water. They'd come up with enough brain-waves recently, it was time to give the little grey cells a holiday, the band could certainly afford it. They were aware that their fans needed time to take stock as well - Queen had given them a lot to think about over the past few years. Freddie, of course, would continue to spice up the gossip columns, as was his wont. In fact, one particular 'Freddie activity' would provide ample entertainment for Queen spectators this year.

For the second year running, they started 1979's touring schedule with a three-month blitz of Europe, leaving behind their No 9 single 'Don't Stop Me Now' (from 'Jazz') to hold the fort in England. After a paltry month's break in March, the four workaholics shot off East for their first visit to Japan in three years. Freddie, in particular, was over the moon about this opportunity to swell his collection of Japanese artefacts and, of course, to visit "all those geisha boys and girls" again... On the two-month visit, he fell in love with a beautiful nine-foot lacquered Japanese piano, which subsequently found itself shipped back to Freddie's home in Kensington, London. When Freddie and piano would make contact was anyone's guess for, as if on auto-pilot, the band trotted straight back into the studio (Musicland in Munich) in June to piece together what was to become their first live album - a travelogue of their 1978/79 world tour.

The band had splashed out on recording fifty shows in their entirety throughout Britain, Europe, Japan and the States between October 1978 and May 1979. Picking out twenty-two numbers, the resulting album, entitled 'Live Killers', was released in July 1979. Predictably, it raced up to No 3. The accompanying single, 'Love Of My Life', unfortunately did not do so well - remaining static at No 63 it was, and would be, the only single that didn't reach the Top Forty.

There was one track in particular on the album that caused some consternation, not just amongst the public and press, but the band as well. Roger Taylor wasn't happy with the album anyway, but he was particularly concerned about the inclusion of the pre-taped 'Bohemian Rhapsody', which the band never played live. Whilst a backing tape provided the music, the band would leave the stage. Brian counteracted:

"'Rhapsody' is not a stage number. A lot of people don't like us leaving the stage. But to be honest, I'd rather leave than have us playing to a backing tape. If you're there and you've got backing tapes, it's a totally fake situation. So we'd rather be upfront about it and say 'Look, this is not something you can play onstage. It was multi-layered in the studio. We'll play it because we think you want to hear it.'"

Fair enough. How could Queen release a representative live album without including their most remarkable composition? But still, it also begs the question: did Queen introduce backing-tapes into live music?

Whilst in Munich, the band also started work on songs for a new studio album. This was a little premature, because the next album wasn't due until the following year - 'Live Killers' would keep their fans happy until then. But the four work addicts appeared to need their annual dip into the studio. As it turned out, they were so relaxed in Musicland, with all the time in the world to create a masterpiece, that they ended up writing far too much material. Only four of the tracks recorded during the summer of 1979 actually made it onto the final vinyl, 'The Game': 'Crazy Little Thing Called Love', 'Save Me', 'Sail Away Sweet Sister' and 'Coming Soon'. The rest would be stockpiled for future use. But they did make an interesting discovery during those early sessions - Rheingold 'Mack' Mack, their engineer, was turning out to be quite a talent on the desk, and the band decided to credit him as their 'co-producer' on the studio album (Roy Thomas Baker was now totally out of the picture). It was a role he would grow into, and excel at over the years, going on to produce such luminaries as T-Rex and David Bowie. All thanks to Queen.

On 18th August, Queen played their first European gig in over a year. But the open-air festival at Saarbrucken Ludwigparkstadion did not run as smoothly as it should have done. Topping the bill over Rory Gallagher, Ten Years After, Molly Hatchett, The Commodores, Lake and Red Baron, Queen's set was so riddled with technical problems that Roger Taylor, in an uncharacteristic fit of frustration, trashed his drumkit at the end of the show. Fortunately, he wasn't using his beloved matt black Ludwig kit that night!

It wasn't Roger's year at all. Dissatisfied with the live album, aggravated by technical hitches and, to cap it all, he couldn't even have a holiday without some disaster occurring. During a well-earned vacation in St Tropez that September, Roger's treasured Ferrari blew up and burst into flames, frying everything inside but

Roger, who managed to escape in the nick of time. But there was more. Still in the South of France, Roger was out on the water one day whizzing around in his motor-boat, when the engine died. Miles off-shore, he spent three hours aimlessly drifting around before being rescued. He only wanted a holiday!

An exhausted and dejected drummer joined up with the rest of the band in Montreux in October. They'd decided to buy Mountain Studios for themselves. When resident engineer David Richards asked Freddie why Queen wanted the studio, he said: "To dump it in the lake dear..."! They could afford to do whatever they wanted.

On 5th October, Queen released one of the four tracks recorded at Musicland. The rockabilly-flavoured 'Crazy Little Thing Called Love' was such an irresistible, quirky little number that it shot straight up to No 2. The accompanying video featured a gang of scantily-clad girls ripping at Freddie's t-shirt - ironic for a man who was, by now, aware of his demon sexuality. The single was written by him:

"I wrote 'Crazy Little Thing Called Love' in the bath. I actually dragged an upright piano to my bedside once. I've been known to scribble lyrics in the middle of the night without putting the lights on."

Roger: "'Crazy Little Thing Called Love' - it's not rockabilly exactly, but it did have that early Elvis feel, and it was one of the first records to exploit that. In fact, I read somewhere - in 'Rolling Stone' I think it was - that John Lennon heard it and it gave him the impetus to start recording again. If it's true - and listening to that last album, it certainly sounds as if he explored similar influences - that's wonderful."

Freddie, meanwhile, had been exploring a more personal influence. He had long been a ballet fan, and it was his dream to actually perform in a proper, classical ballet. He'd often been heard to exclaim: "When I saw Baryshnikov onstage, I was so in awe I felt like a groupie."

On 7th October, Freddie's dream came true. After taking a crash-course in ballet and mime, he was invited by Derek Dean and Wayne Eagling of The Royal Ballet to dance with them for a charity gala at the London Coliseum. He had the time of his life, dancing his heart away to specially-orchestrated versions of 'Bohemian Rhapsody' and 'Killer Queen'. It wasn't the first time Queen's material had been 'classiced up': in 1977, the London Symphony Orchestra had released their own classical version of 'Bohemian Rhapsody' as a single, and for inclusion on a 'Rock Classics' album. But this was different. The ballet version was unusual, to say the least, and an ever-faithful Roger Taylor, who managed to sit through the whole experience, thought it was *dreadful*. Freddie, of course, disagreed, and described how he felt waiting in the wings for his first-ever pirouette: "I was very brave, but I really enjoyed the experience with the Royal Ballet Company. I don't know how those ballet people do it - the same steps every night! I couldn't perform within that framework."

"I was shivering in the wings with nerves. It's always much harder when you are put outside your sphere, but I always like a challenge. I'd like to see Mick Jagger or Rod Stewart try something like that."

After the show, another of Freddie's dreams came true - meeting Royalty. Prince Andrew was backstage and wanted to meet the notorious singer-cum-ballet dancer. A nerve-wracking evening all-round!:

"I was wearing a white scarf and holding a glass of wine when I was introduced to Prince Andrew. But I was so nervous, I didn't realise my scarf was dangling in the drink. There I was trying to be really cool and suddenly the Prince said, 'Freddie, I don't think you really want this getting wet.' He squeezed out the scarf and that broke the ice between us."

"I said, 'Thank goodness you've put me at ease. Now I can use the odd bit of dirty language'. Then we both burst out laughing. He really got into the spirit of things and even had a dance. He's really quite hip in those sorts of situations. I have a lot of respect for Royalty. I'm a tremendous patriot."

Though Queen were indulging in the rewards of their wealth and fame, hob-nobbing with Royalty and racing about in flash cars, they hadn't forgotten their fans. Aware that they hadn't played an 'intimate' gig for years - only arena concerts where they appeared as tiny matchstick men on a distant stage - they embarked on a 'Crazy Tour' of Ireland and England in November and December, in support of the 'Crazy Little Thing Called Love' single. But that wasn't the biggest surprise. After Odeon/Apollo-size gigs in, amongst others, Ireland, Birmingham, Liverpool and Brighton, Queen prepared for their 'Crazy Tour Of London'. The band were looking forward to returning to their roots, for they would be playing the club circuit! The Lyceum Ballroom, Tiffanys in Purley, the Mayfair in Tottenham, the Lewisham Odeon...

The mini-tour was great fun for everyone but the police, who experienced major headaches trying to quell the mass hysteria caused by Queen's arrival at some of London's minor establishments. So riotous was the crowd waiting at Oxford Street's HMV store for Queen's instore signing on 12th December, that the Met forced the band to cancel their visit at the last minute. The traffic build-up was horrendous.

There were other problems with these mini gigs - like how to cram Queen's equipment, however slimmed down, into these inadequate venues. Roger recalled a particularly amusing incident at the Lyceum on 13th December:

"I remember at the Lyceum the roof was too small to fit in all our lights. So we asked the manager if it would be OK to drill two holes in it! He was fine about it, as long as we paid for the holes! Then we got a call from Paul McCartney saying Wings were playing there next week and they'd need a hole in the roof too, so could he pay for one of them? Just think - we became the first ever group to sell Paul McCartney a hole..."

With business heads like that, no wonder Freddie, Brian, Roger and John were the highest-paid directors in Britain!

For once, the press had been remarkably unscathing about Queen this year - even, surprisingly, Freddie's fling with the Royal Ballet. Maybe they hadn't quite believed such a story could be true. And their attitude to the 'Crazy Tour' was actually quite humble. After all, how could they criticise the band for so obviously considering the needs of their fans? Brian:

"We thought it was important to actually visit people again. Unless people can see you in their hometown, it can almost seem like you don't exist. It's also a relief to us because, having done the big barns, it's nice to be somewhere where people can actually see and hear you.

"The advantage of what we're doing this time is that, because our sound and light systems are better than ever, we can really knock audiences in the stomach. The only real disadvantage is that not everybody can get to see us - but I think that those who do, have a great time. It's great fun, too, because the reward is much more immediate. In the larger venues you tend to lose that intimacy, but on the other hand you gain something else. You get a feeling of an event, and the more people there are, the greater the tension becomes. As a result it makes you work harder, particularly to reach the people at the back.

"I doubt very much whether we'll be going back to large venues in England, because there aren't actually many good ones. Bingley was quite good, but it's dirty and nasty for the people who come to watch. The NEC in Birmingham was the same - and it was definitely far too big. It's nice to do those sort of places once and see what they're like, but there aren't many we'd want to go back to. I wouldn't want to do Earls Court again, nor Wembley, and it's quite possible that after doing Alexandra Palace we won't want to do that. But it's worth a try, because we're trying to do some special things with Ally Pally. We wanted to do one big gig in London to sweep up all the people we couldn't otherwise cover."

The Ally Pally gig on 22nd December was a major success, a kind of welcoming home of the prodigal sons. The atmosphere was warm, friendly - and reassurance for Queen that they were still very much loved in their home country. Four nights later, on Boxing Day, they rounded the year off with a gig at the Hammersmith Odeon, part of a week of 'Concerts For The People Of Kampuchea'. Queen were the only band to play an entire set - but others who participated in the week's gigs were Paul McCartney and Wings (as The Beatles had failed to reunite for the event), The Who, The Specials, The Clash, Ian Dury, The Pretenders, Rockpile and Elvis Costello. Queen's whole set was recorded, but only one track, May's 'Now I'm Here', appeared on the 'Concerts For The People of Kampuchea' compilation, which would be belatedly released in April 1981.

1979 had been a fairly low-key year, but one in which Queen had, at last, given themselves a chance to look over their shoulders at a career that seemed to have reached its peak. The 'Crazy Tour Of London' was warm nostalgia for the band and their longer-lasting fans, who hadn't been in *close* contact with each other for nigh on five years. Having gathered their whole career into one train of thought, they were now ready to get down to some serious work again. Time to finish 'The Game'.

1980 was going to be busy. Queen would be spending almost the entire year away from England, touring extensively round the States and Europe before returning home at the end of the year. But first, 'Save Me', from the Musicland sessions last year, was released as a taster for the new album. Whether or not it was representative of the rest of 'The Game' was a mystery even to the band as the album was nowhere near completion! Whatever, the single reached No 11 before its release date on 25th January on the strength of advance orders. The memory of Queen's 'Crazy Tour..' was still lingering.

By February, 'Crazy Little Thing Called Love' had reached America's ears via import copies played on the vast network of radio stations - and topped the U.S. charts. It was a perfect introduction for the album, which would be released in July to coincide with Queen's sprawling American tour.

But, of course, they still had to complete 'The Game'. Between February and May the band were, once more, immersed in Musicland with Mack, their ever-blossoming co-producer. But it wasn't just the new album they were working on...

In April 1979, Queen had been approached by film producer Dino de Laurentis about writing the score for his remake of the 1930's classic science-fiction series 'Flash Gordon'. The band had been suggested to de Laurentis by a mutual friend. "But who are the Queens?" the film producer had remarked in bewilderment, being a man with little rock'n'roll knowledge.

At the time, the band had turned down the offer. They were on the verge of touring Japan again, and had a studio album to think about. But de Laurentis had left the offer open, impressed by Queen's massive array of credentials. Queen, in turn, had been spurred into action by watching a portion of the completed movie. Brian:

"We saw twenty minutes of the finished film and thought it very good and over the top. We wanted to do something that was a real sound-track. It's a first in many ways, because a rock group hasn't done this type of thing before, or else it's been toned down and they've been asked to write pretty mushy background music, whereas we were given the licence to do what we liked, as long as it complemented the picture."

So, in May 1980, in between recording sessions for 'The Game', they started work on their most unusual project to date. It would take them a total of six months to complete, at sporadic sessions in various studios in the U.K., Europe and the States as they toured around the world.

'Flash Gordon' was a whole new ball-game to Queen. Although they decided to release it as their next studio album, after 'The Game', they had to keep in close contact with those involved with the film as well. Thus director Mike Hodges and musical arranger Howard Blake oversaw the whole album process. So, much as 'Flash Gordon' was treated as a band project, with Brian co-ordinating and producing, Queen also had to ensure it was appropriate as support for the film's action. Tricky, but as usual, they were capable of tackling anything! After the album's release in December 1980, the band would reveal that their main influence for the sound-track had been Zither and Zaza's extravagant filmscore for 'Prom Night'. Whether or not this admission was tongue-in-cheek is anyone's guess...

Meanwhile, having finally completed 'The Game' in May, the band took a little precious time off to taste the delights of private life. Roger, in particular, was having better luck this year than last and, in June, his long-term girlfriend, Dominique, gave birth to a baby boy, Felix. At first, it seemed that the 1979 jinx was following him, because Felix was born two months premature and weighed in at only 2lbs (equivalent to two bags of sugar!) but, after close observation, he grew as healthy as any normal baby boy. The question on everyone's lips was - would Roger and Dominique get married? The drummer's terse reply put paid to to any more speculation:

"Dominique and I won't get married because of the baby. We don't need to."

In the meantime, Freddie was keeping the tongues wagging. What was he doing with Elton John at a party in the House Of Commons sponsored by Arts Minister Norman St John Stevas? The press had stopped speculating. It was beyond them. Ever since Freddie's ballet episode, Queen hardly seemed worth sharpening their pencils for... or were they?

They hated the single, 'Play The Game', released on 30th May. They hated the album (released 20th June) even more. The single reached No 14, the album No 1 (their first since the two Marx Brothers' albums). But even Queen's fans were concerned that the band were selling out. For the first time, there was no quaint inscription on the sleeve boasting 'no synths'. The band were blatantly exploring new territories again. They'd done it before with 'News Of The World' and 'Jazz', but this time, they seemed to be boldly going where, perhaps, they didn't belong. Roger was now playing synthesiser, and John, usually such an unassuming influence, had introduced a funk/disco element into Queen's repertoire. The Deacon-penned 'Another One Bites The Dust' was an instant hit on both sides of the Atlantic when it was released in late August: No 7 in the U.K., No 1 in America, where the baseball team The Detroit Lions immediately adopted the single as their anthem - and promptly lost their next five games! Still, the single would become 'Best Single Of 1980' at the American Music Awards Ceremony in 1981, awarded 'Top Crossover Single' by Billboard, and was to be Queen's biggest world-wide selling single to date. But, despite the single's success, John was getting a lot of flack for taking Queen in this funky direction. Creem magazine were quoted as saying: "The bass line on 'Another One Bites The Dust' is lifted straight out of Chic's 'Good Times' as if the Sugarhill Gang had never existed."

John wasn't amused, but said nothing to that particular magazine. He was not about to be baited into a marathon slanging match - it just wasn't his style. He did, however, explain the origins of the single:

"I listened to a lot of soul music when I was in school and I've always been interested in that sort of music. I'd been wanting to do a track like 'Another One Bites The Dust' for a while, but originally all I had was the line and the bass riff. Gradually, I filled it in and the band added ideas. I could hear it as a song for dancing but had no idea it would become as big as it did. The song got picked up off our album and some of the black radio stations in the U.S. started playing it, which we've never had before."

It came as no surprise to the rest of the band that John had come up with such a pop-orientated song. It'd happened before. His first composition to appear on a Queen album had been 'Misfire' off 'Sheer Heart Attack', which had a decidedly poppy edge to it. And there was the lightly commercial 'You're My Best Friend' off 'A Night At The Opera'. Brian:

"I think 'You're My Best Friend' is amazing. John went out completely on a limb to do that. It's not the kind of thing we'd done before but he knew exactly what we wanted."

But Brian wasn't, at first, as confident about 'Another One Bites The Dust'. It seemed to be a total departure even for Queen:

"It's funny, it's a different world. Initially it was very hard for me to come to terms with it because when I started growing up as a guitarist, all the guitar-playing I wanted to get away from was that soul stuff. I felt I didn't want the guitar to be a backing instrument. So my first reaction was to say that I didn't want to play it. But then as you become more exposed to it you see it in a different light.

"Gradually, I became accustomed to it and realised that there was something there, even though I'd rejected it for a few years."

By the time the single came out, the band were already two months into their Stateside tour, where 'The Game' had become their first chart-topping album. In Canada, the album had turned platinum an unbelievable *seven* times! It hardly seemed to matter what the press either side of the Atlantic said: Queen's unpredictability only seemed to bring them more popularity. Unlike any other long-serving group, they continued to cock a snook at consistency, breeding familiarity through their seemingly limitless flexibility. If they'd stuck by the same formula all these years, they'd only have been criticised for having a blinkered attitude. The fact that they couldn't win either way gave them the perfect excuse to do whatever they wanted! Brian explained Queen's attitude to the constant media badgering, which had now been going on for nearly a decade:

"There are lots of little mechanisms built into the relationships between a musician and the press, which means - almost inevitably - that you fall out. But it happened very early to us, so perhaps it doesn't apply. Generally, I could write the reviews of our albums, the good ones and the bad ones... It's a very limited view of what goes on, as soon as something becomes successful, it can't be worth anything. I did think in the beginning it was important to keep the lines of communication open, to talk to everybody. In the end though, after many experiences, you find that it really doesn't come out. If the guy has stated already that he hates you, and can't see anything in you that is worthwhile, then nine times out of ten, if you spend your time trying to convince him how good you are, he goes away and writes what he thought anyway! We do have a reputation for not wanting to talk to people, which is really not that true most of the time, if we have time we'll always talk. But if somebody slags you off in a way you don't think is fair, you don't want to talk to them again."

One angle that nobody had bothered to work on was that Queen were probably the most observant and broad-minded band since The Beatles. They watched and listened with respect to each interesting new musical vibe, and worked a little of each into their own regal structure. Based on a robust foundation of their own, it was as if Queen were building a massive wall of different-coloured bricks, gathered from all sorts of places. The wall was growing taller and taller every year.

Of course, there were bricks that just didn't fit into the scheme of things. John's funky attitude had been a real gamble, but had somehow worked. But Roger Taylor had ideas in his head that he felt were not a part of the great Queen structure. Since his wayward single, 'I Wanna Testify', in August 1977, the seeds of a solo album had been growing. During a two-week break in the American tour, he somehow managed to cram in some studio time to work on his solo project, 'Fun In Space'. The album wouldn't be released until the following April: "There isn't enough room on Queen albums for a lot of the things I want to do, so I'm expressing my own excess."

Naturally, as soon as word of Roger's lone venture reached the press, all hell broke loose again. And later in the year, when Roger played drums on Gary Numan's 'Dance' album, it was apparently confirmation of a division in the ranks. Queen splitting up! Roger sick and tired of the rest of the band! It'd all been heard before. Fortunately Queen's fans were now so used to the media's shit-stirring that they discarded the rumours as inconsequential pap. The volatile rows between band members were now a part of Queen's appeal, not a sign of impending doom. Most relationships stand in the midst of a certain amount of crossfire. Brian explained how illogical it would be for Queen to break up:

"We've had some pretty heated arguments over the course of our career, but we've learnt how to stop. We don't get to the point of blows any more as we did a few times in the past. We know each other well enough to know which way the argument's going to go. A lot of things can be unsaid yet understood.

"I think each of us thinks of leaving quite a lot. But we all know that, even though we might get our own way if we left, we'd still lose something. We'd lose more than we'd gain at the moment. It's a stimulating environment and because we don't always agree it's good for us.

"Think about it - if you split up, then you lose your vehicle. It has a certain balance of talents, a name which people identify with and warrants them giving your records at least one play as opposed to throwing it in the bin. If you look at most people who've split off from a successful group, they very seldom find a situation that's either commercially successful or personally satisfying. Getting your own way doesn't always make you happy in the end. We always fight, we always have done, but in the end it's been good for us all."

The break-up rumours would continue for the rest of Queen's career, as each member of the band indulged in the occasional throes of independence. There'd be solo albums, there'd be contributions to other people's projects, there would even be total departures from the course of rock'n'roll - but Queen would never split up. They were like four cylinders who couldn't work efficiently without each other.

In any case, their solo projects never interfered with their commitments to Queen. The band always came first. Roger's little affair with independence was strictly worked around Queen's 1980 American tour.

This year, Queen seemed to have peaked in America too, playing not one, not two, but three consecutive nights at New York's prestigious Madison Square Gardens. Brian noticed the rise in Queen's stature since their last visit:

"You're really progressing when you get to play Madison Square Gardens for one night, then two, then three. You're reaching more people each time, and it's a recognition that the people who enjoyed themselves the first time have come back and brought their friends. It's a good feeling to build all the time but getting bigger is not the be-all and end-all. Often if you sell more records, it doesn't mean that the quality of the record is any better."

Returning from the States in October, the band spent the next two months completing the 'Flash Gordon' sound-track. By now, they'd decided to stall the release of their 'Greatest Hits' album until the following year. 1981 would be their official Tenth Anniversary anyway, so it made more sense. 'Flash Gordon', then, would be Queen's second album of 1980. Another gamble, but at least this time everyone would know that the album was intended as a sound-track as well.

The single, 'Flash', was unleashed on 24th November just as Queen were starting their European tour. Although not at all Queen in essence, it rose to No 10. Taking a break from Europe for a few days, they took in their only British gigs of the year, two at the 11,000-capacity Birmingham NEC on 5th and 6th December, three at Wembley Arena from 8th to 10th. As 'Flash Gordon' had just been released - on the 8th - the band incorporated the new album's material into their set and, to add a little sci-fi spice, Freddie was carried onstage for the encores by Stars Wars villain Darth Vadar! Queen were back in full glory. Brian talked at the time about the band's live appeal, and their unerringly loyal fan brigade:

"We do have a lot of power. We just hope we can divert it in the right direction. I know it looks like a Nuremberg Rally, but our fans are sensible people, they're creating the situation as much as we are, it's not that we're leading them like sheep.... You just play music which excites people, which interests them. It's rock'n'roll, there's no philosophical reason why we should be there.

"Touring is certainly the most immediately fulfilling part of what we do, and it's not really a big strain - mentally or physically - because we're well organised, we know how to do it. All you have to worry about is playing well on the night. For me, it's by far the best part of being in the band. Suddenly life becomes simple again!"

Queen's career to date had not been simple, but it had certainly been lucrative. By the end of 1980, against all odds Queen had sold 45 million albums and 25 million singles. It was a record, an incredible feat for a band who, a decade ago, had played their first gig at the College of Estate Management in front of a mighty audience of eighty! The following year, Queen would break all previous records by playing before 131,000 rock'n'roll-starved people on one single night...

CHAPTER TWELVE

WE ARE THE CHAMPIONS
1981-1982

*"It's a long time since we've felt such warmth from a
new audience, although we couldn't see much because
of the size of the crowd. We feel really good about it
now, as if our ambitions have been partly realised
again."*
(Brian May)

1981 was Queen's Tenth Anniversary, the year
they pulled out all stops in their mission to reach
as many people as possible with their music.
Queen's British fans, unfortunately, suffered a
severe lack of their favourite band all year. They
were so busy conquering the world, there was no
time for celebrations, no time to crack open the
champagne or spare a few nostalgic moments with
those at home. In fact, the only acknowledgement
of Queen's decade of decadence was the 'Greatest
Hits' package EMI would release in November
1981. Britain would see neither hide nor hair of
Queen for almost eighteen months...

The band were, in fact, taking their
mammoth show to a race of people
who'd never been exposed to rock'n'roll
before, so they should never have been accused of
abandoning England - they were, to their credit,
meeting the needs of thousands of less fortunate
fans. After nipping over to Japan for five
consecutive nights at the legendary Budokan in
Tokyo, Queen and their large family of crew and
equipment flew to South America in mid-
February. The flight from Tokyo to Buenos Aires

is one of the longest direct flights in the world, incidentally!

Queen had first decided to visit South America about nine months previously when it was becoming more and more evident that their music was reaching, and being appreciated in that wild and poverty-stricken part of the world. Despite the destitution in Argentina and Brazil, 1979's 'Love Of My Life' had become a massive success there. The band felt it was time that such a neglected part of the world should be rewarded for their undeniable faith in the band, and for their love of rock'n'roll in general. The whole operation, nicknamed 'Gluttons For Punishment' (indeed!), would be a great challenge - enormously expensive, dynamically and technically complex - but Queen were determined to do it. A sense of adventure set in and, it had to be said that Queen were, literally this time, boldly going where no band had gone before....

The tour - involving six stadium concerts in Argentina, two in Brazil in February and March, followed by a further three in Venezuela and four in Mexico in September and October - had been immaculately planned. The main problem to be addressed was that Argentina and Brazil had never hosted a major concert before, so there were no technical facilities for such an event. No such thing as 'equipment hire' for example. The network co-ordination involved in transporting equipment from various depots in America, England and Japan to Buenos Aires was of labyrinthine complexity. In an army-type exercise, twenty tons of sound equipment were shifted from Tokyo (in a stretched DC-8 cargo plane), forty tons from Miami, as well as sixteen tons of stage scaffolding from L.A. The latter alone cost

£40,000 to set in motion. Queen's five tons of lights (four hundred and sixty-five overheads) represented a full six months' production at an airport light factory in the States, and burnt 300,000 watts of power. But there was more.

Queen had been booked to set up their concerts in some of South America's most legendary football stadiums. Knowing how sacred their football turf was (is!) to them, Queen had to work out a way of holding these massive concerts, minimum capacity 30,000, maximum 131,000, without disturbing the earth. From the South American authorities' point-of-view, they could be about to play host to a series of riots - they didn't want to be responsible for condoning the desecration of their holy football turf as well! The whole idea nearly fell through at that point, until somebody came up with a brainwave. After much research, it was deemed possible (if not practical) to move three tons of artificial grass/astro turf from California to South America by plane. An extraordinary feat, but it was done.

Why? Was the question on every cynic's lips. What were Queen getting out of all this? The satisfaction of breaking several records? Being the first to break through seemingly impossible barriers? Money? The latter was laughable: each day of that South American tour sapped £25,000 from the band's budget.

Before visiting that uncharted territory, they may have been motivated by the challenge of it all, a desire to achieve something nobody else had. But afterwards, it was a very different story. "It's been a long time since we've felt such warmth from a new audience..." Brian May had said. "I really felt Freddie was communicating with people all the way to the back row..." marvelled Roger Taylor. 479,000 impassioned Latinos, starved of rock'n'roll, suddenly presented with a feast - an overdose - of entertainment. From 28th February to 21st March 1981, Queen experienced something unique: the power of humility. A nation of people reaching out in raw gratitude for giving them such a precious gift. Most moving experience of all was the sight and sound of thousands of South Americans heartily singing every single word of their favourite Queen number, 'Love Of My Life'. In return, Freddie, moved almost to tears, whispered the word 'obrigado' into his microphone: 'Thank you'...

From 30,000 people at Mar De Plata in Argentina to that extraordinary 131,000 crowd at Morumbi Stadium in Sao Paulo, Queen couldn't have failed to please if they'd tried. The statistics were impressive enough: the first group ever to tour outdoor stadiums in South America, and to play to as many as 479,000 people; the first to fill three nights in a stadium in the same city - Buenos Aires, in front of 164,000 people; the first ever to be broadcast live on television coast-to-coast in Argentina and Brazil - to a staggering 35,000,000 people; and, of course, the band who have drawn the largest-ever paying audience in the world, in Sao Paulo. Forty miles of electrical cable, twenty-five different companies involved in the whole operation, ninety flights with twenty-five different airlines to carry all personnel to South America, one million pounds-worth of insurance for all equipment... But, at the end of the day, Queen were not impressed by their own statistics. It was the people that left the most lasting impression on them, as Freddie recalled:

"We were really nervous. We had no right to

automatically expect the works from an alien territory. I don't think they'd ever seen such an ambitious show, with all the lighting and effects. They looked so...enthralled."

Roger expressed a more objective view of the experience:

"In a way I was surprised that we didn't get more criticism for playing South America. I didn't think we were being used as tools by political regimes, although obviously you have to co-operate with them. We were playing for the people. We didn't go there with the wool pulled over our eyes. We fully knew what the situation is like in some of those countries, but for a time we made thousands of people happy. Surely that must count for something?"

"We weren't playing for the government, we were playing to lots of ordinary Argentinian people. In fact, we were asked to meet the President, President Viola, and I refused... (The rest of Queen did meet the President). I didn't want to meet him, because that would have been playing into their hands. We went there to do some rock music for the people."

The ecstatic and emotionally drained band ended the first leg of their South American tour at the end of March. During Queen's visit, their Argentinian fans had shown their undying appreciation for the band by buying enough Queen product to ensure a Top Ten position for every one of their albums! Saying farewell for the time being to their new-found Latino friends, they flew off in different directions for a well-earned break. Whilst Roger and Brian flew directly back to London by DC10, Freddie decided to fly by

Concorde. Although this meant having to change at Paris, Freddie was just pleased to be able to travel in comfort and style on the most expensive-possible journey back to England! John, meanwhile, snuck off to New York on his own.

As the band made their way to their various destinations, the first fruits of Roger's solo sessions in Switzerland the previous year were beginning to see the light of day. 'Future Management', the first single off 'Fun In Space', was released at the end of March. It only reached no 49, and the second single, 'My Country', unleashed on 29th June, flopped completely - but the album, out on 6th April, peaked at 18:

"Afterwards I was so mentally exhausted that I couldn't even be trusted to select the single. There were certain things I wanted to do which weren't within the Queen format; in a way it's like flushing out your system, and until you've done it you just don't feel fulfilled. If I get more ideas for songs I might eventually do another solo thing, but Queen would always get priority.

"The title 'Fun In Space' doesn't mean that the album should be regarded as 'Son Of Flash Gordon', but in many ways it is nostalgic, capturing the old days when life was perhaps a little more uncertain. I've got some old sci-fi books and magazines which I browse through from time to time. Maybe there are things up there in space watching us. I wouldn't find that surprising at all."

'Space' seemed to be the theme of the year. From July to September, the whole band immersed themselves in their own Mountain

Studios to start work on their tenth studio album, 'Hot Space'. If 'Jazz' and 'The Game' were regarded as eclectic, 'Hot Space' would confound even Queen's most broad-minded critiques.

Whilst they were working at Mountain, John Deacon's old friend David Bowie happened to be taking refuge in his Swiss home. Accepting an invitation from John to visit the band at Mountain, David dropped in... And next thing he knew, he was recording a song with them. 'Under Pressure', from 'Hot Space', was sprung on an unsuspecting public on 26th October 1981. It shot straight to No 1. David Bowie recalled, in bewildered tones, the spontaneous jam that turned into a top-selling single:

"They turned up in Montreux, so I went down to the studio and we just started one of those inevitable jams, which led to a skeleton of a song. I thought it was quite a nice tune, so we finished it off. It sort of half came off, but I think it could have been a lot better. It was a rush thing, one of those things that took place over twenty-four hours. I think it stands up better as a demo. It was done so quickly that some of it (the lyric) makes me cringe a bit, but I like the idea."

Roger was much more positive about the single: "It's one of the very best things Queen have ever done, and it happened so casually... As long as we can continue to do this, and surprise even ourselves, we'll carry on."

With the release, on the same day as the single, of the Queen Tenth Anniversary 'Greatest Hits' package - a compilation album, a 'Greatest Flix' compilation video and an official 'Greatest Pix' book - the band were soon topping the album, singles and video charts. How many more records could Queen break?

In the meantime, the band had returned to South America in September to take in the second stage of the 'Gluttons For Punishment' tour. More of the same unadulterated passion.

The band had particularly fond memories of the final gigs, in Pueblo, Mexico. Upon arrival at the Estadion Cuahtermoc, they were appalled to find that the stadium looked like it'd been hit by a bomb. Filthy, strewn with litter and rubble, with plumbing and lighting that defied description. The crew worked hard to clear up the site and, by the day of the first of four gigs, the Cuahtermoc probably looked better than the day it was first opened! The ever-efficient roadcrew had even painted appropriate signs around the site.

The organisation had been going like clockwork, and it seemed that the Cuahtermoc's resident security team were co-operating accordingly when they were seen to search fans entering the stadium. Confiscating batteries from tape-recorders, the band were relieved that there'd be no bootleg material of the Pueblo concerts. Wrong. Once inside the stadium, fans were greeted by stallholders selling batteries at hugely inflated prices. The scam was easy. The batteries they were selling were from the security guards' haul of confiscated units!

After a couple of gigs in Montreal, Canada on 24th and 25th November, Queen returned to England - the blinding success of the 'Greatest Hits' package guaranteeing a warm welcome home. Meanwhile, The Royal Philharmonic Orchestra and Royal Choral Society were laying foundations for an event that would ensure Queen exited 1981 in the most magnificent style yet. On 8th December, they performed a selection of Queen's material for a Royal Promenade Concert at the Royal Albert Hall. The concert, broadcast on 28th December, was held in aid of leukaemia research. A great honour for Queen - establishing them as part of the pride of the United Kingdom, not just a best-selling rock'n'roll act. Freddie summed up the year thus:

"As long as we feel a sense of achievement and that we are breaking new ground, like doing the South American tours, we're happy, and we ought to continue."

The first two months of 1982 were spent putting the finishing touches to 'Hot Space' in Germany. As with 'The Game', the band were not bound to any tight schedules - with the 'Flash Gordon' album pushing the 'Greatest Hits' compilation back to the end of their Tenth Anniversary year, there was no rush to fill any void. Having finished, they flew to Los Angeles for a short break, and then in April, returned to England to sign a new long-term, five-album contract with EMI.

Beginning 1982's world tour in April, Queen spent two months hurtling round Europe, starting in Scandinavia, and ending in Munich on 21st May. Their choice of Bow Wow for the support slot was adventurous, and proved that Queen were as open-minded as they claimed to be....

'Body Language', the second single off 'Hot Space', was released on 19th April, only reaching No 25, but the album itself, on sale four days later, managed to make it to No 4. But 'Hot Space'

certainly confused everyone. Queen's audience
had been growing more and more diverse every
year but, with this album, the market appeared to
be limitless. Obviously, the transient Queen army
would've bought the album as a matter of course,
but the band seemed to be aiming at a
funk/dance/disco audience too. 'Hot Space' was
massively pop-orientated. The press had pretty
much given up trying to suss Queen out, generally
accepting them for their eclecticism. The Record
Mirror review of the album was positively
glowing: *'New styles and a whole new sense of values.
You'll love 'Hot Space.'*

Obviously, there were still the hard-core critics
who were not at all amused by Queen's
'experimentation' techniques, claiming that 'Hot
Space' would do them no favours at all. The
general train of thought from this more cynical
quarter was that the band were merely wandering
around in a void, with no direction. It did seem
that way. Queen's more traditional fans, those
who still maintained that 'Sheer Heart Attack' was
the band's best album, did start to fall by the
wayside (somewhat dismayed by Queen's overt
display of commerciality) to be replaced by the
more 'hip' dance-floor generation. Perhaps the
band could've progressed a little more gradually,
and taken it a mite easier on their older fans.
Keeping up with the times is always a good move,
but there's also such a thing as completely turning
your back on the past. Brian attempted to explain
the general drift of the album:

"'Hot Space' is an attempt to do funk properly.
It has a style of playing where you get in and get
out quickly, hence the title 'Hot Space'."

A rather lame description. Maybe the band

weren't too sure about the album themselves. It could almost have been guaranteed that Brian, advocator of the more traditional hard rock sound, had been out-voted this time around, particularly by Freddie's leanings towards the more disco-orientated market, and John's pre-occupation for funk. Roger would probably have gone along with anything - he'd already expended his personal frustrations on 'Fun In Space'. But Brian was, and always would be, a rock fan, pure and simple.

'Hot Space's chart position was no real indication of the public's opinion of it - there were enough habitual Queen record buyers to bolster the success of any album they released, whatever it was like. Obviously, if they were to put out too many dubious albums, their fan-base would begin to tail off, but for the moment at least Queen were safe. The next album, however, would have to be given a great deal of thought, lest they lose their direction completely. As Freddie pointed out once:

"If we put out a terrible album, people *wouldn't* buy it."

Nevertheless, having brought the album out, they had to serve up the element of 'Hot Space' for the rest of the year, to promote the damn thing. After the European tour, Queen paid their British fans a visit for their first live appearances in the U.K. in eighteen months. The band had had to cancel two gigs, at Manchester's Old Trafford and London's Arsenal football ground, due to 'lack of toilet facilities', as all portable chemical toilets in the country had apparently been hired by the visiting Pope John Paul II! However, both concerts were substituted: the former by their first British gig on 29th May at Leeds United football ground, the latter by the last of the four concerts, at Milton

Keynes Bowl on 5th June. The Leeds appearance was particularly memorable - a return of the prodigal sons, who evidently hadn't been out of their fans' minds at all while they'd been away. The release of the Latin-flavoured 'Las Palabras De Amor (The Words Of Love)' on 1st June had certainly helped (it ambled up to No 17). So, too had 'Queen Medley' - the album of The Royal Promenade Concert last December, which was released around the same time. 40,000 Queen fans turned up to watch their heroes at Leeds, supported by Heart, Joan Jett and The Teardrop Explodes. At Milton Keynes, 37,000 showed up for the concert, which was recorded by Channel 4 television for broadcasting on the first edition of 'The Tube' on 7th January 1983. After that last gig, the band threw an 'end-of-tour' party at the Embassy Club in London at which all guests were expected to turn up wearing either shorts or suspenders and stockings! The 'lig' cost a mighty £10,000.

Meanwhile, 'Las Palabras De Amor' - a more traditional rock ballad - was causing consternation in certain quarters. Although the single was obviously a big thank-you from Queen to their South American fans, the timing had a lot to be desired because, in June 1982, the vicious Falklands Conflict had just begun between Britain and Argentina. Freddie's use of the Spanish language throughout most of the song was regarded as insensitive to say the least. Yet the band themselves were terribly distraught when the war broke out. Having made such communication inroads into that part of the world, to suddenly be torn apart from a country they'd got to know so well, was no less than a personal tragedy for Queen. When the misunderstanding had been cleared up, Freddie was asked for his opinion on the War:

"It's our young men killing their young men. There's no glory in being blown to bits."

Roger remained positive: "We were still Number One in Argentina when that stupid war was going on. We had such a fantastic time there, and that can only, ultimately, be for the good. Music is totally international."

After the controversy had blown over, the next single from 'Hot Space' was released, in August. A disappointing No 40, 'Backchat' was nothing to write home about.

The band, meanwhile, were off round the world again. In the States, where 'Las Palabras...' had been substituted by 'Calling All Girls', the band were, as usual, greeted with hysterical abandon. It must've been almost tedious for the band! From July to September, they travelled throughout America, before ending the year back in the Land of the Rising Sun (more Japanese artefacts and geisha boys and girls for Freddie!).

1982 hadn't been a particularly memorable year for Queen. 'Hot Space' had distanced them from their long-term fans, who were suddenly left wondering where Queen were coming from. The band had a lot of thinking to do and, as such, they decided it was time to take a break from each other for a while - to take stock, and try to regenerate some of the urgency they'd lost over the past year or so.

CHAPTER THIRTEEN

UNDER PRESSURE
1983-1985

*"We were getting too close to each other, getting on
each other's nerves, so we decided to give ourselves
some breathing space...*

*We're totally against apartheid, but I feel we did alot of
bridge-building in South Africa"*
(Brian May)

1983, Queen's year of rest: from each other, from the public eye, from work. The latter, of course, none of them could entirely do without - and yet, working on anything outside the Queen environment was a holiday in itself. Brian explained the reasons why they all needed a break from each other:

"We needed to give ourselves some breathing space. So we agreed to go off and do individual things, so that we could come back to Queen when we actually felt motivated. We took about five months off work, up until August this year. During that time we met and talked a lot, but we didn't actually do anything.

"There's always been a lot of tension within Queen, because we don't like the same things as far as music is concerned and have to find common ground. We often disagree about how things should be presented. We're all very forthright and different. We are very stubborn, but there is a democracy. Nobody has a bigger share of the say than anybody else. But sometimes it's very tense and very hard. It's not the touring, though. That's the best and easiest part. You have to go out there and be as good as you damn well can be. But the thought of doing another album just didn't appeal to us after the last tour, so we thought it was no use forcing it. Better to wait until we'd something to offer.

"We didn't want to split up because we felt that's a mistake so many people have made from The Beatles onwards. It would have been so good if they could have held together for longer. No matter how talented the individuals are, the group is always something more than its components. And we think Queen is an example of a proper group. With all its shortcomings, I think it's worth keeping together.

"After all the fights, we still tend to come up with things that have been through the sieve and are worthwhile - *because* of all the fighting. We still care. We've experimented a lot in the past and some of the experiments didn't work. Our last album was one big experiment and a lot of people totally hated it. And it didn't sell very well - not compared to earlier stuff, anyway. We've had ups and downs. People don't realise that. They think Queen can't do anything wrong. They think we can just stick out an album and it's easy for us. But really it's not. There are varying degrees of success, and we are always conscious that our next album may also be our last. We don't like to repeat ourselves, so there is always the chance that people will hate what we do.

"It's funny. Everyone thought Queen had this big master plan to conquer the world, but really we were so excited just to make an album - that was the ambition in itself. None of us knew what was ahead."

Roger claimed a more fundamental reason for the temporary separation: "After touring America, Europe and Japan we were totally knackered, so we thought we deserved a bit of a rest... It also had a lot to do with the last album not doing as well as previous LPs. We realised that it hadn't been what a lot of fans wanted or expected from us, so we thought a break would give us the opportunity to think things through a bit."

Of course, rumours of a permanent split abounded, but Freddie put their fans' minds at rest:

"I used to think we'd go on for five years, but it's got to the point where we're all actually too old to break up. Can you imagine forming a new band at forty? Be a bit silly, wouldn't it?

"The reason I personally needed a rest was because I just got tired of the whole business. It got to be too much. I decided I really needed a long break. I'd just bought an apartment in New York, and I wanted to spend some time there.

"I don't think we'll ever split, it would seem like cowardice. I suppose if people stopped buying our records, we'd call it a day. And I'd go off and be a strip-tease artist or something!"

Brian also put paid to any split-up rumours:

"People have been rumouring that Queen are going to split up for the last eight years at least. I've got some great cuttings at home from people saying 'One thing is certain, Queen will no longer exist in a year's time'. And that was in 1973!"

John's statement was succinct, to say the least: "We've reached the point where we're working a little bit less as a group."

So, off they went in their separate directions - spending time with their families, as well as getting involved in off-shoot projects. Brian, after getting to know his eighteen-month-old daughter, Louisa (his second child), whom he'd hardly seen at all since her birth, put his production talents to good use with Scottish rock band Heavy Pettin' in the summer. He enjoyed the challenge of working on something other than his own band. The album, 'Lettin' Loose', was recorded, with Mack's help, in London and Munich and released in October 1983. During recording sessions, the band convinced Brian to check out Sheffield metal band Def Leppard, bred from the NWOBHM, and currently riding high with their third album 'Pyromania'. He took their advice. Whilst in L.A. in September recording Queen's eleventh studio album, Brian ventured down to the L.A. Forum one night to see Leppard during their U.S. tour:

"I was bowled over by them. Just amazing. Their show was one of the highest-energy things I've ever seen. They destroyed the place. I went back and told 'em so, and they invited me to play with them the next night. I was highly flattered, so I went on and played a song with them at the end, which was great fun."

At the same time, Brian also contributed some guitar to two tracks on Jeffrey Osborne's album, 'Stay With Me Tonight', at Mad Hatter Studios, Los Angeles. And, somehow or other, in amongst all his other 'holiday' activities, he also found the time to get his own project together. Back in 1981, he'd wistfully stated:

"I'm into paradoxes. I wanted to make an album about them, but the group told me I was a pretentious fart. They were right..."

In the early part of 1983, he had the opportunity to explore those 'paradoxes'. The 'Starfleet Project' EP was, explained Brian, "just a jam", he insisted it wasn't intended as a commercial venture and ignored the press' cries of 'self-indulgence' when it was released on 31st October. The three-track, thirty-minute EP only reached No 35, the single, 'Starfleet' (used as the theme tune for a Japanese children's programme of the same name) remaining static at 65. But Brian wasn't worried. After all, hadn't he, himself, stated that "...most people who've split off from a successful group...very seldom find a situation that's either commercially successful or personally satisfying..."?.

The lengthy blues 'jam' was dubbed 'Brian May And Friends', the friends being Eddie Van Halen, Phil Chen, REO Speedwagon's Fred Mandell and Alan Gratzer, with a little backing-vocal help from Roger:

"To be honest, I didn't even know if I could play with other musicians. I had been so long with Queen I thought, 'What kind of musician am I?'. I had been working the machine, but maybe I had become too much a slave of it... Edward and I took a break from recording and started talking about how it was in the old days when Eric Clapton was doing his thing with John Mayall. We all found 'The Beano' album had been a big influence on us - remember, the one with Eric reading the comic on the cover? It was a classic collector's item for every guitarist. It sounded like they were having so much fun they couldn't stop... 'Blues Breaker', which takes up all of side two on the album, is my favourite part of the record. It seemed very indulgent putting out a long jam but, having listened to it, I think it's worthwhile... 'Starfleet' is rock blues with all the mistakes left in."

Brian was hardly aware that he, himself, was a 'legend' in his own right. As such, he was interviewed by Radio One for their 'Guitar Greats' series. The hour-long broadcasts featured indepth interviews with such legendary guitarists as Jeff Beck, Pete Townshend and Eric Clapton. Suddenly, everyone wanted a Brian May 'Red Special' guitar for themselves. It was impossible for anyone to create something so unique, but still, when Guild guitars asked Brian if they could build a 'Brian May' model, he concurred:

"We've got together and talked about it. They've been through the guitar, taken it to pieces and measured it up, and they reckon they can make something which is very close to the one I made myself all those years ago. Now, hopefully, there should be a Brian May guitar which sounds like my one."

Well, the Guild BBM-1 did sound a little like the 'Red Special' but there would never be a guitar quite as remarkable as that 'May & Son' custom. Larry DiMarzio even attempted those inimitable May pick-ups as well, but they didn't quite catch the magic of the originals. In later years, Brian spoke on the subject of copies:

"A lotta manufacturers have tried to figure out how to make copies. Basically, the copies that came out have come quite close to the original. But is it really necessary for a guitarist to play a guitar that carries another guitarist's name? I would never do that. You can't just copy me by buying a copy of my guitar or a copy of my pick-ups. Naturally, all guitarists have someone who's inspired them. Eric Clapton was the guy who really influenced me, but I don't sound anything like him. Nobody's discovered yet what a horrible style of playing I actually have. I use quite thick strings and I used to use an old sixpence as a plectrum. It's not surprising I suppose how often the strings gave up the ghost. Every guitarist has his way of doing things."

As does every vocalist. Freddie was also getting involved in various projects. 'Dropping by' Michael Jackson's house one day, he and the great recluse actually recorded a couple of songs together in Michael's home studio - but nothing has ever been released from that session. Freddie persisted in his attempts to draw Michael into another project for years after that:

"Michael has been a friend of ours for a long time. He's been to our shows and enjoyed them. We make a great team.

"I'd like to release something with Michael, because he is a really marvellous person to work with. It's all a question of time because we never seem to be together at the same time. Just think, I could have been on 'Thriller'. Think of the royalties I've missed out on!"

A couple of years later, having still been unable to pin Michael down, Freddie stated, disappointedly:

"Michael Jackson and I have grown apart a bit since his massive success with 'Thriller'. He's simply retreated into a world of his own. Two years ago, we used to have great fun going to clubs together, but now he won't come out of his fortress. It's very sad. He's so worried that someone will do him in that he's paranoid about absolutely everything."

Meanwhile, both Freddie and Roger had got together to help out Billy Squier on his 'Emotions In Motion' album, singing backing vocals on the title track at the sessions in Musicland Studios. The sessions had turned out well - and the relationship would be repeated three years later for Squier's 'Enough Is Enough' album.Singing backing vocals was a role Roger was used to playing - in 1981, he'd contributed harmonies to Kansas' 'Vinyl Confessions' album, and - wait for it - comedian Mel Smith's 'Julie Andrews' Greatest Hits' single, which he'd also produced.

When Roger had joined up with Freddie and Billy, he'd been taking a break from recording his second solo album, with a little help from Status Quo's Rick Parfitt, amongst others. Parfitt and Taylor had been close friends for years, their common interest outside music being cars and motor-racing - and the two, along with Roger's girlfriend Dominique, headed off to the Monaco Grand Prix in May. In typical form, Taylor and Parfitt managed to get themselves arrested, as Rick recalled:

"We just went to Monaco, and managed to finish up in jail! It was quite a funny night - we were accused of something we didn't do, but we sat in prison all night, and it rained all the next day, so we didn't see the race. We had a thoroughly bad time, but we came home laughing!"

John, as usual, was lying low, mainly spending time with his rapidly-expanding family, but he did rear his head a couple of times. In his element playing bass on a single called 'Picking Up Sounds' by Man Friday & Jive Junior, he also helped Roger with his solo album, and - most extraordinary, found himself jamming with tennis players John McEnroe and Vitas Gerulaitis! Obviously, the bass-player had no serious plans for an alternative career...

Of course, whilst the band hadn't physically been in the public eye, their presence during 1983 was being kept well and truly alive through those wonderful media, TV and film. In January, the first 'Tube' programme had been broadcast on Channel 4, featuring the Milton Keynes concert of last year. On 20th August, the same gig was broadcast on MTV throughout America. And in early August, the film, 'We Will Rock You', began its world tour in front of an audience of 6000 at San Diego Sports Arena. The tour would continue in the autumn.

By September, Brian, Freddie, Roger and John were ready to get on with their collective career. Refreshed and unburdened of their respective frustrations, they eagerly bundled into the Record Plant, L.A., where they would spend the next two-and-a-half months. All four were now confident that they had a clear, united vision of the next album's direction, and were not merely churning out the goods. As was their wont when they were feeling particularly clear-headed, and needed to turn over another new leaf, they decided that, once again, it was time to clear out some more dead wood. This time it was Elektra America's turn. On 26th October 1983, Queen swapped over to Capitol

Records in the States, Brian signing a solo deal with the company at the same time. At the great celebratory party, Roger summed up his opinion of the Elektra contract in two inebriated words: "It SHUCKED!".

Brian explained the band's reasons for ringing the changes, and revealed his personal satisfaction with the new album's direction:

"We wanted the next album we made to be in a new situation. We were trying to break from our old record company in America, which was important. We didn't want to deliver another album in that situation. There was that feeling that we might just be making another Queen album and putting it back into the machine. We didn't want that, and it's all worked out very well. We agreed on Capitol, and signed a deal with them. Suddenly we have a company in America that's really excited to be getting their first Queen album.

"I think our new album is damn good, much better than anything we've done for a while. It's going to be called 'The Works'. And it really is! There's all the Queen trademarks. Lots of production, arrangements and harmonies.

"I always got the most enjoyment out of the harder material, and the new album is a lot harder...but I did fight to get it that way. We've done some fantastic over-the-top harmonies and a lot of heavy things that we haven't done for years.

"The pressure has always been against me, because not everyone in the band is into the same stuff as I am. I get the most pleasure out of things that I can hammer down and get some excitement out of. Basically, I'm like a little boy with the guitar, I just love the fat, loud sound of it. But that's not important to the others, and I agree with this, the songs come first. That's where the common ground ends and the arguments begin. The result is always a compromise."

It all sounded very promising...

But what on earth was 'Radio Ga Ga'? A deliberate attempt to totally alienate their more rock-orientated fans? All the assurances from the band that their new material was harder, tougher, a return to their former glory, appeared to some people to be a sham. When this apparently banal, Taylor-penned single was released on 3rd January 1984, it did goo-goo its way to No 2, and it was a Queen-atypical anthem, but the lyrics were enough to make the poppiest chart-watcher cringe. Soon, however, critics and fans alike realised that there was a lot more to 'Radio Ga Ga' than at first met the eye. It was, for a start, heavily sarcastic, and wholly tongue-in-cheek, aiming its cynical arrows at the commerciality and crassness of radio. The accompanying video was impressive to say the least. Queen had somehow managed to get permission to use some of the original footage from the legendary 1926 Fritz Lang movie, 'Metropolis'. Utilising the grand old black-and-white film - with its sinister '1984' type connotations - as a backdrop, the band were seen as part of the film, blending into, and zooming around its massive city-scapes. Roger explained where he'd got the idea for 'Radio Ga Ga', and how the band had come across 'Metropolis':

"One day, the radio came on in my house and my three-year-old son Felix came out with 'radio poo poo'! I thought that sounded good, so I changed it around a bit - first it was 'radio ka ka', then I came up with 'Radio Ga Ga'. The song - that chorus-line - came after I'd locked myself in a studio for three days with a synthesiser and a drum machine.

"As for the video - I'd been watching a lot of MTV in America, and it seemed to me there was far too much emphasis on a band's visual image". (An ironic statement, as Queen had pioneered the idea of 'band videos' in the first place!). "I basically wanted to put that across in the video. Giorgio Moroder had bought the film rights to 'Metropolis'..." (from the German authorities) "...and he wanted us to write a song to go with it. We wrote him a song and we swapped it for the rights to use some footage from the film. It's a great movie, and I'd always been interested in using images from it. There's a sense of nostalgia in watching a silent film that links in watching with the nostalgic view of radio I got from remembering nights spent listening to Radio Luxembourg under the bedclothes."

So *that* was why Moroder, the film producer of 'Flashdance', had been seen at Freddie's birthday bash in L.A. in 1983... What Moroder precisely wanted from Queen, in return for using 'Metropolis' for their video, was a contribution to the sound-track for his revamping of the original movie, which was to be released later in the year. Freddie would be the one to come up trumps.

In the meantime, 'Radio Ga Ga' could not quite fight its way to the No 1 slot. There was a certain, controversial obstacle sitting obstinately in Queen's way. Frankie Goes To Hollywood's 'Relax' had been spicing up the charts since

November 1983, and didn't seem to be going away. Of course, the fact that Frankie (led by the sexually-questionable Holly Johnson) were none-too-subtlety advocating the cause of homosexuality with 'Relax', was enough to cause the press to compare some members of the band to Freddie. Their angle was something akin to: Gay Protagonists Dominate Charts!

For God knows what reason, Freddie agreed to give the Sun (of all tabloids) an exclusive interview. Unaware that their angle would be aimed at his recent revelation: "Oh yes, I'm gay, I've done all that", he innocently walked into the interview, assuming this was merely a chat about Queen's return to the arena. The final piece, published in February, was a grubby little exposé, which revealed more about the reporter's character than anything else. Freddie was appalled:

"I was completely misquoted. But from the beginning, the press have always written whatever they wanted about Queen, and they can get away with it. The woman who wrote that story wanted a total scoop from me and didn't get anything. I said, "What do you want to hear? That I deal cocaine?" But for God's sake, if I want to make big confessions about my sex life, would I go to The Sun of all papers to do it?! There's no fucking way I'd do that. I'm too intelligent."

A little while later, speaking on the subject of the outrageous, androgynous Boy George of Culture Club, Freddie was more cautious: "He's a great talent. That boy is so brave," he said, careful to add, "One of my big fans is Boy George." by way of putting his views into perspective. Boy George was just a friend. And, just to emphasise that his respect for the extraordinary creature was based purely on professional interest, he expanded:

"When I started off, rock bands were all wearing jeans, and suddenly here's Freddie Mercury in a Zandra Rhodes frock with make-up and black nail varnish. It was totally outrageous. In a way, Boy George has just updated that thing, the whole glam-rock bit. George is more like a drag queen. It's the same outrage, just doubled."

Freddie, of course, had shed the skintight leotard years ago, in favour of a more - well - camp image: the black moustache and black leather cap, hot-pants and vest. Yes, he was definitely dressing like a homosexual, he was definitely *bisexual,* but so what? Was his music less brilliant because of it? No. Was he a danger to society? No, although Freddie's bisexuality *would* ultimately prove a danger to himself. For the time being however, his sexuality was nobody else's business but his own:

"People can think what they like about my bisexual stage image. That's what I want them to do. I want to keep the mystique."

Woefully shaking his head at the press' unbelievable ignorance and downright lack of respect, Freddie joined the rest of the band - and Culture Club, Bonnie Tyler and Paul Young - for the San Remo Annual Song Festival in Italy at the end of February. Oddly enough, this was Queen's first performance in Italy. Thirteen years of touring, and somehow or other, they'd missed the land of great opera and dramatic gestures. The festival was almost a disaster, with Brian and Roger scratching each other's eyes out over material, the stage - and anything else they cared to bring up. But Freddie, in that inimitable way of his, dragged them out of their lousy moods, and had them both in stitches in no time at all. The row was probably a result of tension from the long lay-off. It was taking them longer than expected to get back into the swing of things, as Roger surmised:

"It's strange how rusty we are, and so we're trying to blow the cobwebs away. It's taking a lot of work."

On 27th February 1984, 'The Works', the eagerly awaited eleventh album, was released. Their first album for two years splashed into the charts at No 2, instantly turning gold. Queen had returned!

But, during the early months of 1984, the band still kept their heads down, rehearsing hard, because the latter part of the year would be riddled with gigs. Queen were planning another large-scale operation, but one that would prompt a great deal of criticism and controversy - not just from the press this time, but from their peers too...

On 14th April, the irresistibly quirky 'I Want To Break Free' was released, its accompanying video causing much hilarity in Britain, and much concern in some states of America, where it was subsequently banned. Featuring the band dressed as different Coronation Street characters (Roger's idea), the inevitable sniggers were aimed, in particular, at Freddie and Roger's characters. Freddie, with moustache intact, decked out in suspenders and stockings, stilettos, huge false boobs and black wig; Roger, dressed as an extremely convincing, very pretty schoolgirl! Queen seemed to be bringing irony and humour into their make-up as well as everything else. For once, the press were speechless, and some reporters may even have smiled a bit (you never know).

In May, the band broke away from rehearsals in Munich to 'perform' at the Montreux Golden Rose Pop Festival in Switzerland. The event, on 12th May, earnt each band a mere £2000, but its TV coverage was worth ten times that - broadcasting to an incredible 400 million viewers world-wide. But Roger's opinion of the event was none too complimentary:

"All things like that are farces, coz you're miming to playback.Freddie made it pretty obvious he was miming. But, you know, 400 million viewers...who could say no?"

Back in Munich, Freddie began work on his own solo album, spurred on, no doubt, by Roger and Brian's projects. Initially, studio work was delayed, as Freddie got himself involved in a night-club brawl on 22nd May. Beaten up and badly kicked, he tore a few ligaments in his leg and was ordered to rest for a while.

Roger's second solo album, meanwhile, finally saw the light of day in June 1984. 'Strange Frontier' showed much more maturity than his debut, and struggled to a creditable No 30. The album included versions of Bob Dylan's 'Masters Of War' and Bruce Springsteen's 'Racing In The Streets' apt for a car fanatic). Freddie co-wrote one track, 'Killing Time', Rick Parfitt colluded on another, 'It's An Illusion', which featured John Deacon on bass. Unfortunately, the two chosen singles did not do as well as the album: 'Man On Fire' stuck at 66, and the title track failed to chart at all. Still, Roger was the first of the band to even chip the outer casing of a secondary career.

In July, Queen's single 'It's A Hard Life' slithered up to No 6, pushed on its way by a video of extreme decadence and gluttony! And thenQueen made an announcement that sent shock-waves around the country. They were going to play the notorious Sun City Super Bowl in Bophuthatswana, South Africa that October. The news was not received well. Sun City was a gambling complex which was run on its own insidious apartheid terms - and part-financed by the South African government. Any band daring to play that oasis of luxury in the midst of township squalor was accused of insensitivity and ignorance. Still, not even a blunder like that could affect the attendance during Queen's European and U.K. tours in August and September, which included four blinding Wembley Arena shows. After the first of two nights at Birmingham NEC in September, the band received a letter from the management congratulating them on a record single-night merchandising turnover - a staggering £51,414.50! At the same time, the band were nonchalantly shattering another record - nine Queen albums in the U.K. Top 200 at the same time. No other band had achieved such a feat.

During the tour, Freddie's first single, 'Love Kills', plucked from the Giorgio Moroder-ised 'Metropolis' sound-track album, surprised even Freddie when it reached No 10. Other artists featured on the October-released album included Pat Benatar, Bonnie Tyler, Loverboy, Billy Squier, Jon Anderson and Cycle V.

Leaving the U.K. with the live 'We Will Rock You' video compilation, Queen headed off to their controversial Sun City gigs at the beginning of October. Eight mammoth concerts "played for the people", not for any political reasons, as Brian stated:

"We've thought about the morals of it a lot, and it's something we've decided to do. This band is not political, we play to anybody who comes to listen. The show will be in Botswana in front of a mixed audience."

The shows were, of course, a great success, but the band were still being plagued with criticism months after they'd returned. There were differing views of the South African visit even amongst the band members themselves. John tried to communicate the band's abstention from all things political:

"Throughout our career, we've been a very non-political group. We enjoy going to new places. We've toured America and Europe so many times that it's nice to go somewhere different. Everybody's been to South Africa, it's not as though we're setting a precedent. Elton John's been there, Rod Stewart, Cliff Richard. I know there can be a bit of a fuss, but apparently we're very popular down there... Basically we want to play wherever the fans want to see us."

Brian, meanwhile, thought it best to emphasise that Queen totally abhorred apartheid (which, unfortunately, contradicted John's claim that Queen always tried to keep away from political viewpoints):

"We're totally against apartheid and all it

stands for, but I feel we did a lot of bridge building. We actually met musicians of both colours. They all welcomed us with open arms. The only criticism we got was from outside South Africa."

Roger was the only one who admitted to a certain concern about the South African concerts, whilst still managing to sit firmly on the fence!:

"In a way I do regret playing. But in some ways, I would defend what we did. I mean, basically we play music to people - lots of them preferably - and I think a lot of crap is talked over here about things that people don't really know about.

"'I Want To Break Free' is an unofficial anthem among the African Congress Movement, and 'Another One Bites The Dust' is one of the biggest selling songs in South African black history."

But still, Queen's copy-book was forever blotted - literally, it turned out, as they found themselves on the United Nations' cultural blacklist....

Not a particularly resounding exit to 1984. Though the anti-nuclear 'Hammer To Fall', the next offering from 'The Works' seemed to be hinting at a much heavier direction, and reached lucky 13, 'Thank God It's Christmas' wasn't exactly progressive. Specifically released for the Christmas market, the single only just managed to stumble to No 21. As Freddie would say: 'Oh dear'...!

Still, as awards go, the Silver Clef Award from the Nordoff Robbins Music Therapy for

'Outstanding Contribution To British Music' was a damned good indication of Queen's mammoth achievements over their entire career, never mind 1984.

1985 began more positively when Queen played the Rock In Rio Festival on 11th and 12th January. The band never thought they'd beat their first South American trek in terms of audience capacities, but confronting that massive pool of 250,000 people (at 3.00am in the pouring rain) put paid to that idea. The South Americans still had all the words to 'Love Of My Life' firmly glued to their lips! (The 'Live In Rio' video, upon its release in May, would fly straight to No 1.) Still, even Rio wouldn't be able to surpass the magnificent scale of a very special concert in July.

After their debut gig in New Zealand (where the band were confronted by angry apartheid demonstrators outside their hotel), and a string of gigs in Australia and Japan, Queen returned to England to take part in the most legendary rock'n'roll event in history. Woodstock had been the first-ever outdoor rock festival in 1969, and no other festival had come close to encapsulating that pioneering event. But, on 13th July 1985, all that changed. Woodstock was, at last, allowed to rest in peace....

Live Aid was a major landmark. Enlightening billions of people around the world to much more than just the rock'n'roll experience, its sole purpose was to raise money, on a grand scale, for the victims of the Ethiopian Famine. It turned out to be the greatest ever fund-raising event - and gave rock'n'roll a much needed respectable profile. Held live at Wembley Stadium (in front of 72,000 people) and in Philadelphia, Live Aid broadcast some of the world's greatest rock and pop acts to a world-wide audience. Queen emphatically stole the show with their twenty-minute set, which included 'Hammer To Fall', 'Crazy Little Thing Called Love', 'We Will Rock You' and 'We Are The Champions'. Bob Geldof spoke for the majority of people when he enthused:

"Queen were quite simply the best band of the day.."

Although they made a lot of new fans that day, the press accused Queen of simply 'doing it for the exposure'. The suggestion was ridiculous. Although Queen were gaining valuable - global - exposure, (i) so was everybody else and (ii) they hardly needed it. Weren't Queen the great rock'n'roll explorers? Hadn't they plundered countries no other band had even considered? But they weren't alone, for DJ/entrepreneur Jonathan King was busy accusing Geldof of the same thing. Roger was appalled:

"Geldof's whole thing was magnificent. He did it out of the purest motives. I cannot believe arseholes like Jonathan King can denigrate something that's done real good when he's done no good to mankind except litter the planet with dreadful records! How *dare* he? How worthless parasitic specks like him can have a go at something that's so good, I don't know."

Queen had been invited to play Live Aid by their keyboard-player Spike Edney, who also doubled up as trombone-player for Geldof's Boomtown Rats. The decision to play had not been made overnight. Indeed, Geldof had had to fly to Australia for a meeting with Queen's aide Jim

Beach for discussions of the finer details. It wasn't simply a case of saying 'Broadcast world-wide? We'll do it!'. On the contrary. Brian:

"Actually, it was only by a narrow squeak that we got involved in it. Our first reaction was 'Oh God! Not another one!'. We'd been involved in quite a few and we were a bit disillusioned as to how the whole business works."

John continued: "We didn't know Bob Geldof at all. When 'Do They Know It's Christmas' was out, that was a lot of the newer acts. For the gig, he wanted to get a lot of the established acts. Our first reaction was, we didn't know - twenty minutes, no soundcheck...!

"When it became apparent that it was going to happen, we'd actually just finished touring Japan, and ended up having a meal in the hotel discussing whether we should do it, because obviously they wanted our answer, and we said 'Yes'. We didn't get involved in the running order thing, but strangely enough we did well coming on when we did (right after David Bowie).

"It was the one day that I was proud to be involved in the music business - a lot of days you certainly don't feel that! But that day was fabulous, people there forgot that element of competitiveness... It was a good morale booster for us too, because it showed us the strength of support we had in England, and it showed us what we had to offer as a band."

The band lay low for the rest of the year - mainly because they needed the break. But the inevitable rumours arose once more that Queen were on the verge of a split. John had reported "an enormous row" between Freddie and Roger over a Queen boxed set, due for release at the end of the year. A pretty trivial matter, but at least it indicated that the customary Queen fights were still alive and kicking! The band wouldn't be the same without them - at least they weren't ignoring each other.

But the solo projects continued - and multiplied - during this 'resting period', and 'grew ever more plentiful' (as they say in the Bible), so the break-up gossip became a part of daily newspaper life.

Freddie's debut solo album, 'Mr Bad Guy', had come out in April. Not a patch on his work with Queen, but as an interesting little diversion it made its mark on the charts at No 6. Three singles were plucked from the album, but only one, 'I Was Born To Love You', was worth mentioning, reaching No 11 in April. Another track, 'Foolin' Around', was used in the Nick Nolte film, 'Teachers'. Freddie, of course, was immensely proud of his 'baby':

"I've put my heart and soul into this album. It's much more beat-oriented than Queen's music, and it also has some very moving ballads. They're all love songs, things to do with sadness and pain. At the same time, they're frivolous and tongue-in-cheek; that's my nature.

"I've wanted to do a solo album for a long time, and the rest of the band have encouraged me to do it. I wanted to cover such things as reggae rhythms and I've done a couple of tracks with a symphony orchestra. It has a very rich sound."

Meanwhile, in August, Freddie was seen publicly with his new 'escort', forty-two year old German actress, Barbara Valentin:

"Barbara and I have formed a bond that is stronger than anything I've had with a lover for the last six years. I can really talk to her and be myself in a way that's very rare."

Of course, no relationship would ever be quite as rare and precious as his platonic affair with Mary Austin, who was always more than just a constant friend:

"Mary works in my organisation and looks after my money side and all my possessions. She's in charge of the chauffeurs, maids, gardeners, accountants and lawyers. All I have to do is throw my carcass around onstage!"

Thus, the intensity of his relationship with Barbara did not last. Freddie, as usual, blamed it on himself, as he did every time he broke up with someone:

"I seem to eat people up and destroy them. There must be a destructive element in me, because I try very hard to build up relationships, but somehow I drive people away. They always blame the end of the love affair on me because I'm the successful one. Whoever I'm with seems to get into a battle of trying to match up to me, and over-compensating. Then they end up treading all over me! I can't win. No-one loves the real me inside, they're all in love with my fame, my stardom. I fall in love far too quickly and end up getting hurt all the time. I've got scars all over. But I can't help myself because basically I'm a softie - I have this hard, macho shell which I project onstage, but there's a much softer side too, which melts like butter.

"What I really like is a lot of loving. And I spoil my lovers terribly, I like to make them happy and I get so much pleasure out of giving them really wonderful, expensive presents."

Roger, meanwhile, had been busier than any of them. In April, he and Mountain Studios' David Richards had co-produced Jimmy Nail's cover of the Rose Royce hit 'Love Don't Live Here Anymore'. And the Taylor/Richards team continued throughout the year.... Producing an album by Scottish band, Sideway Look... Feargal Sharkey's 'Loving You' single (on which Roger played drums and synths) at The Townhouse and Eden Studios... The debut album by Virginia Wolf... And a single by Camy Todorow, called 'Bursting At The Seams'.

Roger was also one of several guest drummers to contribute to Roger Daltrey's tribute to Keith Moon, titled 'Under A Raging Moon', recorded at RAK Studios in London.... And he contributed drums to 'Too Young' off Elton John's forthcoming 'Ice On Fire' album.

Compared to Roger's mad flurry of activity, John's list looked pretty paltry. In actual fact, he was rumoured to have started his own off-shoot band, The Immortals. Nobody believed it of course, but when the sound-track to the movie 'Biggles' was released in March 1986, a few people were forced to eat their hats, because The Immortals were credited on the album for one track, 'No Turning Back', also released as a single. John would also contribute some bass licks to Elton John's 'Ice On Fire' and his 'Leather Jackets' album of 1986 and, in February 1986, he would collaborate on a single with Errol Brown of Hot Chocolate.

But Deacon, being the only member of Queen who wasn't really a vocalist, found himself at much more of a loose end than anybody else during the band's breaks. His opportunities for solo projects were limited. All he really wanted was to get back within the Queen framework, the environment in which he felt most secure. Unlike the others, he had no burning desire to vent any frustrations on a solo career. During this 'holiday' in 1985, whilst the others were off being creative on their own, John was just bloody bored:

"We're not a group anymore as such. We're four individuals who work together as Queen, but our working together as Queen is actually taking up less and less of our time. I mean basically, I went spare, really, because we were doing so little. I got really bored, and I actually got quite depressed."

Well, he was going to have plenty to think about in a few months' time....When the single, 'One Vision' (from the forthcoming album), was released in November, the floodgates of criticism opened once more. Suddenly, the press were casting their evil eye over the band again. When they accused Queen of cashing in on Live Aid with the single, the band thought they were just being ignorant and bloody-minded again. Until they read the press release that'd been circulated with 'One Vision'. Some foolhardy (and possibly defunct) press officer had decided that the single was 'inspired' by Live Aid, and saw fit to tell the press. The band were horrified, as Roger remembered: "I was absolutely devastated when I saw that in the press. It was a terrible mistake and I was really annoyed about it. Some public relations person got hold of the wrong end of the stick. I went absolutely bananas when I saw that."

Brian was more philosophical: "We do a lot of stuff for charities, but 'One Vision' was a way of getting back to what we're doing, and if we didn't run ourselves as a business, we wouldn't be around for the next Live Aid. We're not in the full-time business of charity at all. We're in the business of making music, which is a good enough end in itself." 'One Vision' reached No 7, and ended up on the sound-track for the film 'Iron Eagle'...

It was turning out to be a very bad year indeed. Two days after the release of 'The Complete Works', that much-squabbled-over boxed set of all Queen's albums, Sun City came back to haunt the band.

On 7th December, Steve Van Zandt's Artists United Against Apartheid project were featured in the NME. Over here on a promotional trip, Sun City's entertainment director Hazel Feldman was quoted as saying: "A return appearance by Queen should not be ruled out."On 14th December, Queen reacted with the following statement:

"Queen categorically state that they have no plans, at present, to return to Sun City, and wish to make it plain that they have a total abhorrence of apartheid."

It was Queen's parting shot of the year.

CHAPTER FOURTEEN

SPREAD YOUR WINGS
1986-1989

"I think we are probably the best live band in the world at the moment, and we are going to prove it...."
(Roger Taylor, as Queen embarked on their final tour)

Over the past couple of years, Queen had not been everybody's favourite band. Rubbing all the right people up the wrong way with their South African expedition, they'd as good as given the press a fully-loaded gun on a silver platter. The Live Aid and 'One Vision' incidents were a different matter. Media fabrication and an unfortunate misunderstanding, Queen were not responsible for the press' small-mindedness, or their press officer's creativity. So they ignored it all, and got back to work.

1986 would be another year of unprecedented live performances. Even more so than before, these would be shows of superior dimension and quality. A fitting way to end their career as a live band...

But first they had an album to release. 'A Kind Of Magic' was greeted with a cavalcade of praise when it was released in June 1986. Preceded by the single of the same name in March (which reached No 3), the album proved that the more Queen were put down, the more they pulled out the stops! Their experiences of the last couple of years certainly hadn't affected their creativity, and the album moved almost immediately to No 1, charting in a further thirty-five countries.

'A Kind Of Magic' was, in fact, Queen's second sound-track album. Most of the tracks were used to accompany the $20,000,000 'Highlander' movie, starring Christopher Lambert and Sean Connery, and director Russell Mulcahy had been delighted when the band had agreed to work with him. He'd first approached them in 1985, and Queen had decided, as with 'Flash Gordon', to make the album their next official project.

Mulcahy, who'd previously only directed pop videos (Duran Duran, Elton John and Ultravox), knew Queen would come up with the goods, but when he heard the final product, he was totally bowled over:

"Queen's music was just right for the film. They have a very keen sense of visuals. They write very powerful, anthem-type songs, and the film needed just that kind of energy. I've always been a fan of Queen's and for a long time have wanted to work with them."

Producer Peter S Davis was just as impressed:

"The incredible thing about Queen's music is that it works in both the period and contemporary facets of 'Highlander'. They are able to blend the two."

The band themselves were over-the-moon with the film, and Roger described 'Highlander' as:

"...a very heavy film. There's some very heavy stuff in the film."

The movie was, indeed, "very heavy", featuring some wonderfully bloody decapitation scenes.... Queen's collaboration with Mulcahy was so successful that he agreed to direct the video for the 'A Kind Of Magic' single. Filmed in The Playhouse in Northumberland Avenue (the former BBC studio where such classic shows as 'The Goons' and 'Hancock's Half Hour' were broadcast), Mulcahy assured everyone that: "The video will please the six to sixty-year-olds, with magic and fantasy like we used to see in the old musicals of Hollywood."

The album itself was certainly bursting with "magic and fantasy", and the band were more satisfied with 'A Kind Of Magic' than any album they'd released in recent years, as John enthused:

"It breathed new life into us. We were planning a long rest, but it so filled us with enthusiasm and ideas that I think we've come up with some of our best material ever."

The next two singles off the album, 'Friends Will Be Friends', released in June, and 'Who Wants To Live Forever' in September, reached, respectively, 14 and 24 in the charts.

Queen were riding high in the popularity stakes again, much to the press' dismay. And, just to rub salt into the media's wounds, the band had held their first International Fan Club Convention on 25th April in Great Yarmouth. Over one thousand fans had turned up, travelling from as far afield as South America and Australia. Queen aide Jim Beach:

"We'd thought of a fan club convention like that a couple of years ago but never got round to organising it. If it works well, I'm sure it will become an annual event."

The band, meanwhile, were still furiously busy with their respective off-shoot projects: Freddie had contributed two tracks to the stage musical 'Time' (created by close friend Dave Clark, and in which Freddie would play a part in 1988), and sang a duet with an obscure person called Jo Dare for the German film 'Zazou'; Roger was producing Magnum's new album 'Vigilante' and would contribute to Elton John's 'Leather Jackets' album (with John); and both John and Brian co-wrote and contributed to an album by some bloke called Minako Honda!

How they were managing to concentrate on their collective career with Queen on top of all this moonlight activity was a mystery to many people. But they were, in fact, plotting some serious concerts for 1986. Their last...

The 1986 European tour started in Sweden at the beginning of June, progressing through Belgium, Germany, Switzerland and Ireland, before returning to England in July for the biggies: at Newcastle's St James Park, Wembley Stadium and Manchester City Football Ground. Queen were really pricking the media's conscience this year: all proceeds from The Newcastle gig, sponsored by Harp Lager, would be going to the Save The Children fund. Jim Beach:

"Queen were so bowled over at the amount of enthusiasm for their shows they wanted to say thank you. Princess Anne's dedication to Save The Children goes beyond the call of duty, and is an example to us all."

Promoter Harvey Goldsmith, meanwhile, could not believe the response to the U.K. gigs. At a press conference at the St James Club, Piccadilly, Goldsmith revealed that the ticket applications for the two Wembley Stadium gigs (on 11th and 12th July, and supported by Status Quo and The Alarm) amounted to almost half a million, and that tickets for Newcastle had sold out in an hour. As a result, he continued, the band would be playing at Knebworth Park on 9th August:

"The queue of ticket applicants at Newcastle was longer than the queue for Cup Final tickets when Newcastle United were in the F.A. Cup Final. The Manchester show was the fastest-selling show ever to be advertised in that city. I've never known anything like it. We were overwhelmed at the demand for Wembley Stadium tickets, but not surprised. We were literally swamped with requests. The reaction was above and beyond any of our expectations. I'm really thrilled. It just shows that, after fifteen years, Queen are bigger than they've ever been. And the rush for the Newcastle and Manchester shows went beyond our wildest dreams." ·

At the first Wembley gig, Queen unveiled their most ambitious stage-show yet. Before the concert, Roger hinted at the magnitude of the operation:

"We are going to play on the biggest stage ever built at Wembley, with the greatest light show ever seen. No-one who comes to see us will be disappointed. We are going to put in at least four weeks of practice - more than we have ever done in our careers. I think we are probably the best live band in the world at the moment, and we are going to prove it."

After the feats Queen had already achieved in their fifteen-year career, they hardly needed to prove anything. But that was the way they were, they would never stop at just equalling a previous record or achievement - they had to totally shatter all expectations. And, at Wembley, they did just that.

The final Wembley gig was filmed by director Gavin Taylor for world-wide television. It was, and still is, a favourite and frequently-aired live concert. The sight of Freddie swanning around the stage resplendent in red and white regal robe and crown is an image that has stayed with Queen's fans forever. Although, after Manchester, Knebworth would officially be Freddie's last gig, that glorious pose, as Freddie held the great crown high above his head and surveyed his 'subjects' at Wembley, has been immortalised on film, and thus became the more familiar of those last concerts. They had, indeed, proved that they were "probably the best live band in the world"!

But there were still countries that Queen hadn't yet conquered. Returning to Europe to continue their 'Magic' tour at the end of July, the band ventured into that unknown territory behind the Iron Curtain. There's no way on earth Queen could've known this year's tour would be their last, but it certainly seemed as if they were indelibly stamping their magnificent presence on 1986, and making sure that every country in the world knew their name.

'The Hungarian Experience' on 25th July was certainly the highlight of Queen's year, and a major landmark in rock'n'roll history.

Sneaking into Budapest via presidential

hydrofoil along the River Danube, Queen were looking forward to teaching the rock-hungry Hungarians all about the live experience of a top Western group. They were expecting to be confronted with bewilderment, maybe shock - certainly ignorance as to Queen's particular specialities. After all, the last Western musician to peek behind the curtain was Louis Armstrong in 1964 - and Queen were the first band *ever* to play a large stadium concert in the Eastern Bloc. But the band were in for a surprise...

Fifteen lorries rolled across Europe to the Nepstadion (built by Stalin) in Budapest, carrying Queen's dimension-defying equipment, including an entire segmented stage that would take a whole two days to be erected by the sixty-man roadcrew; eight miles of cable and five generators to provide adequate power for Queen's light-show, which comprised two sixty-foot P.A. towers adorned with search-lights. The Hungarians wouldn't know what'd hit them!

Yet, when the band looked out at a sight that was so familiar to them, but least expected in that isolated corner of the world, they couldn't believe their eyes: 80,000 Hungarians with their hands raised high in hand-clapping 'Radio Ga Ga' salute, denying all rumours that the Eastern Bloc were totally cut off from Western civilisation. As moved as he'd been in South America, Freddie paid tribute to Queen's Iron Curtain fans by singing one song in halting Hungarian, from words written on his hand! And, as a final, hands-across-borders gesture, Freddie sashayed onstage for the encores swathed in a Union Jack flag, with the Hungarian national emblem embroidered on the back.

Of course, Freddie's penchant for luxury didn't abate even in the drab environment of Budapest. The whole band had been given suites in one of the city's most superb hotels. Freddie, however, had managed to acquire the Presidential Suite, leaving the rest to rattle around their (slightly) less sumptuous rooms. When Roger ambled into Freddie's room one day, and made some off-the-cuff remark about the obscenity of the Presidential Suite, the singer merely observed: "All suites are equal, my dear, but some are more equal than others!". To which Roger snorted: "Well it's a fuck's sake more equal than mine!"

The band had had a wonderful time in Budapest. The whole experience had been filmed for posterity as 'Magic In Budapest', utilising every single 35mm camera in Hungary! Roger described the event:

"We had a wonderful time in Hungary. I think everybody who came to the Nepstadion enjoyed themselves. Specially our support! It was about sixty middle-aged ladies in traditional costume, singing a Hungarian folklore version of 'Jumpin' Jack Flash' and, believe me, it was different!"

Queen ended their European tour in Spain in August. It was while they were in Barcelona on 31st July that Freddie first spoke openly about his love for opera - an obsession that'd first infiltrated Queen's repertoire in 'Bohemian Rhapsody' in 1975. Appearing on a Spanish Arts programme one day, he announced to the nation that his main reason for being in the country was to meet his favourite opera singer, Opera Diva Montserrat Caballe. Little did he know that the great lady herself was watching the TV broadcast, and would shortly be contacting Freddie...

And so to Knebworth, Queen's finale as a live band. Grander than even the Wembley Stadium gigs, the group performed before an audience of 120,000 people on 9th August, their biggest-ever U.K. gig. Utilising a custom-built six-thousand square-foot stage, Queen decided that to place video screens either side of the performing area, as most bands did, would be too distracting. Instead, they demanded that a twenty- by thirty-foot Starvision screen be erected over the stage. This, of course, was easier said than done, but Queen's roadcrew were one of the most efficient in the world, and handled the task accordingly. It entailed some of the most complicated rigging in rock'n'roll history. The crew had to lay concrete foundations in order to mount the twenty-five ton screen securely atop its purpose-built tower, and the tower itself had to be anchored to twenty-five skips of sand ballast. Queen never did things by halves!

That, of course, was true of their after-show parties. The decadent backstage affair at Knebworth boasted a fun-fair, and a fully decked-out wooden-floored ballroom with silk canopy! The band themselves were transported to and from the gig in their own 'Magic' helicopter.

Queen ended the year on a suitably high note by releasing a souvenir of 1986's European Tour. 'Live Magic', encapsulating the - magic - of Wembley, Knebworth and Budapest, shot straight in at No 3. In 1986, Queen had sold a total of 1,774,991 albums in the U.K. It wasn't surprising: over one million people had seen Queen on their European tour, more than 400,000 of those in Britain alone. Not even the press could deny that

Queen were, indeed, The Champions! But, little did anyone know, including the band themselves, that The Champions would soon be bowing out of the arena...

During 1987 and 1988, Queen started to recede from the public eye. There would be no more albums until 1989, no more live shows at all. But there would be plenty of activity from the individual members of Queen over the next couple of years. Freddie, in particular, seemed to be growing more and more intent on a solo career, as was Roger - although the band would continue to deny this signified the end of Queen.

Freddie, being such a larger-than-life character, made a bigger impact than the rest with his solo projects, of which there were two. One was his traditional 'Mr Bad Guy' material, which was a natural offshoot from his role with Queen. His cover of The Platters' 'The Great Pretender', which reached No 4 in March 1987, was accompanied by a video of Freddie in drag. Typical.

But it was Freddie's other project that really caused major shock-waves. Opera Diva Montserrat Caballe, having seen Freddie on Spanish TV in 1986, had gone out of her way to get in touch with the outrageous singer, and the strange partnership arranged to meet up in Barcelona in March. The result of much discussion was a project that totally fulfilled Freddie's dreams. He'd already danced with the Royal Ballet, now he was about to dabble in a little opera. But, where his ballet fling was merely a one-off flirtation, Freddie's interest in opera seemed to run deeper.

First, he decided to write a song about

Barcelona, titled, coincidentally, 'Barcelona'. The resulting collaborative single, an odd mixture of rock and opera, was eventually released in October, reaching No 8. A tuxedoed Freddie and the Diva were seen to heartily blast forth the song at the Ibiza Festival at the legendary Ku Club in May, an appearance that resulted in the Spanish Olympic Committee's decision to use the song as the 1992 Olympic anthem. Fair enough - a one-off single, no big deal. But then it transpired that he and Montserrat Caballe were working on a whole album together! What the rest of the band made of *that* was anyone's guess. However, John at least agreed to help out a little on the project. Entitled, naturally, 'Barcelona', the album wouldn't be released until October 1988. At that time, Freddie and Montserrat perform 'Barcelona' before the King and Queen of Spain, as they closed the massive 'La Nit' event, held to celebrate the arrival of the Olympic flag from Seoul. Freddie, shortly after the Ku Club appearance, oozed with respect for Montserrat Caballe:

"I've liked her for years. It's like a dream come true working together."

Roger, meanwhile, was busy laying the foundations for his own band, The Cross, the formation of which he announced in August '87. Using previously unknown musicians from 150 auditions, the band comprised Clayton Moss on lead guitar, Peter Noone on bass, Spike Edney playing keyboards (not entirely unknown of course!) and Josh McCrae playing drums. So where did Roger fit in? As vocalist and lead guitarist of course... That piece of news in itself was enough to raise a few eyebrows! Roger spoke about The Cross shortly after their formation: "The superstar syndrome of getting famous musicians together is just a trap. It's why Sting's lost it with his new album. This is a real band to be taken on its own merits and to succeed or fail by them. The last thing I'm going to do is trade on the Queen thing."

To fail was unfortunately what The Cross were about to do - at least, for now. One of the fruits of rigorous studio sessions was the single 'Cowboys And Indians', released in October. It flopped. Dramatically. Apparently, there weren't enough Queen fans out there willing to condone Roger's solo career yet. The single crawled to No 74, and subsequently staggered out again a week later. Two more singles failed to even make it that far. The album, 'Shove It', was finally released in February 1988, and would've been regarded as a 'Top 60' album had there been such a thing (it maintained a vigil at 58 for all of two weeks). Roger was not perturbed - he had, of course, been through it all before. He enjoyed the challenge of starting again, zooming up and down the M1 in the back of a transit, eating in motorway cafés (well, maybe not!). Taking the band out on their first European tour in support of the album, the return to all the old club and university gigs of yesteryear was obviously great fun, and hugely nostalgic for Roger. At least he was exercising more humility than Freddie, who seemed to be escalating some palatial staircase to ultimate luxury!

Freddie's birthday bash in September 1987 was bombastic. So were all his parties, but this was particularly magnificent. For his 41st birthday, Freddie flew eighty of his friends to Ibiza by DC9 jet, where they were delivered to 'Pikes', one of the island's most exclusive hotels. The party boasted just about everything: flamenco dancers; a twenty-foot long birthday cake carried by half-a-dozen Spaniards decked out in white and gold; and, most impressive, a fireworks display which flashed Freddie's name in lights across the sky! Decadence personified.

And yet, this kind of party was a rare occasion in Freddie's life by that time. The gossip column inches were reducing day-by-day, reports of *'who Freddie was with last night'* dwindling rapidly. Not because the press had suddenly turned respectable, and chose to leave Freddie's private life alone - good heavens, what a miracle that would've been - no, he simply didn't appear to be as much of a party animal as before. The playboy seemed have grown up, at last. In a rare interview Freddie gave around the time of his birthday in 1987, he signified a complete turnaround of his views on sex:

"I lived for sex. Amazingly, I've just gone completely the other way. Aids changed my life. I have stopped going out, I've become almost a nun. I was extremely promiscuous, but I've stopped all that. What's more, I don't miss that kind of life. Anyone who has been promiscuous should have a test. I'm fine. I'm clear."

Gone were the sweeping "I'm a good lay" advertisements of yesteryear, the boasts that "my sex drive is enormous". This was a much humbler Freddie, a man who had been forced to face up to reality in some way. Whether he knew he had Aids at that stage, or was just affected second-hand is not known. But certainly, the Aids toll had begun to affect his immediate circle of friends as long ago as 1985. Close friend, thirty-five-year-old courier Tony Bastin, had passed away then. In 1988, another of Freddie's friends, Nicolai

Grishanovitch, also died, at which point the singer took another Aids test, which apparently proved to be negative.

Anyway, whilst Freddie was trying to realise all his dreams with the help of Montserrat Caballe, Brian was busy getting involved in a couple of inconsequential projects. Apparently spotting a vocal talent from watching actress Anita Dobson on TV's 'Eastenders', he decided to back her attempts at pop stardom. She'd already had a hit in 1986 with 'Anyone Can Fall In Love', the vocal version of the 'Eastenders' theme, and now Brian was going to co-write, play on, sing on, and produce her album, 'Talking Of Love'. It was, really, complete drivel, and failed to register anywhere, although the single of the same name managed to sneak in at 43, briefly, in July 1987. Brian's partnership with Anita continued away from the studio.

Brian's next venture was even worse. Why he agreed to get involved in such a dreadful parody of his own band's most legendary hit nobody knows. But 'Bohemian Rhapsody' was the song that the Comic Strip's spoof band Bad News had chosen to take the piss out of, and they wanted Brian, and the rest of Queen, to help. The resulting single, with John and Roger helping out with the 'Galileos', was appalling, not particularly funny, and thankfully only made it to No 44 in September 1987. Freddie wisely stayed away.

On the Queen front, it appeared that nothing was happening at all during '87 and '88. But, in between solo projects, the band had spent 1988 gradually building up songs for what would be their thirteenth album, to be released in 1989. And, during the long lay-off, their name had been kept very much alive with the odd compilation release, and the inevitable awards. In November 1987, 'The Magic Years', a trilogy of documentary-type videos directed by the Torpedo Twins from Vienna, had been released, and at the end of the year, the band were inundated with the usual truckload of awards. That year, they'd been presented with the Ivor Novello Award for 'Outstanding Contribution To British Music', the American video and film festival 'Silver Screen' award for 'The Magic Years', and the IMMC Award at the Montreux Golden Rose TV Festival.

The end of 1988 was less prestigious. As far as the public were concerned, Queen might as well have split up, for the only event remotely connected with the band was The Cross' performance at the Queen Fan Club Christmas Party on 4th December. At that party, it was announced that Queen had sold more than eighty million albums world-wide by the end of 1988. The event, at the Hammersmith Palais, 'guested' John and Brian, but there was no sign of Freddie. Still, that gig was a sign that Queen would be returning very soon.

In May 1989, Queen surprised everyone by suddenly leaping out of the woodwork with 'The Miracle', their thirteenth studio album. The shock catapulted the album straight to No 1. However, the expected tour did not happen , and the media started to speculate about Freddie's health, in the light of the deaths of his close friends. Their 'fears' were unfounded - at the time - as the videos for the five singles off the album - 'I Want It All', 'Breakthru', 'Invisible Man', 'Scandal' and 'The Miracle' - boasted the same arrogant, energetic Freddie everybody knew. The video for 'The Miracle' was probably the most memorable of all, featuring the band playing alongside 'mini-clones' of themselves!

'The Miracle' charted everywhere, and the more its prestige grew, the more people expected the band to return to their customary, mammoth touring schedule. Queen claimed they were too busy with other projects, and in truth Brian, in particular, was certainly running with the pack. He contributed to Holly Johnson's 'Love Train' single, Living In A Box's 'Blow The House Down', Black Sabbath's 'When Death Calls' from their 'Headless Cross' album and Lonnie Donegan's 'Let Your Heart Rule Your Head', which he co-wrote for the legendary British blues pioneer's 1989 album.

But there was more. Brian was feeling in a particularly charitable mood this year. In June, after hearing the plight of young leukaemia victim Denise Morse, who'd died in February '89, he decided to re-record 'Who Wants To Live Forever' with two specially-chosen children on vocals. All proceeds went to the British Bone Marrow Donor Appeal.

In the summer, both Brian and Roger were part of a team of rock musicians, including Ritchie Blackmore, David Coverdale and Bryan Adams, involved in the Rock Aid Armenia project, set up to help the victims of the Armenian earthquake of 1988.

Roger, incidentally, had somehow ended up producing the single 'Dancerama' for outrageously commercial pop-rockers Sigue Sigue Sputnik. Some of their outlandish behaviour must've rubbed off on him, because the day after his 40th birthday party in July, Roger made the headlines for confusing the Ministry Of Defence, the media and his neighbours. The lasers scanning the sky throughout the party were mistaken for UFOs!

Freddie, meanwhile, had been keeping his head down. After becoming godfather to Mary Austin's little boy, Richard, he dashed off to Switzerland for a rest in mid-1989. Whilst there, he visited Mountain Studios' resident producer, David Richards, and ended up laying down a few tracks. Out of that session came 'Delilah', a quirky little number (written about one of his beloved cats) that would end up on the next album.

By Christmas, the rest of the band had joined Freddie to commence work on what would be the last Queen album....

CHAPTER FIFTEEN

THE NIGHT COMES DOWN
1990-1991

"Freddie was in a great deal of pain (during recording sessions for 'Innuendo'), *but he carried on working because that's what he enjoyed. Working also helped him to have the courage to face his illness."*
(Mary Austin)

1990 was a year of careful recording and cautious activity. The press found that any attempts to get close to Queen were thwarted, and the only statements made by any of the band were succinct and defensive. Looking back, it's clear to see that Brian, Roger and John were deliberately closing ranks around Freddie, to protect him from prying eyes for by now, it was certain that Freddie was ill. When somebody did manage to ask Brian if Freddie had Aids, he categorically denied it, but admitted that the singer's health was "quite rough". That's all anybody was going to get, it would not have been fair on Freddie to usurp his privacy. Naturally, with no solid input, the press filled the void with a totally unfounded campaign of *'Freddie Mercury Has Aids'* stories.

In truth, the band were enjoying each other's company more than ever as they popped in and out of Mountain Studios, which had, by now, become a second home. 'Innuendo', co-produced with David Richards, was being recorded at a deliberately relaxed pace.

This was going to be the last album, so it had to be special. But they were also carrying on as normal, and that included diving off every now and then to fulfil individual obligations.

Brian's most auspicious project to date was his contribution to The Riverside Studios' production of 'MacBeth', which was finally staged between 14th November and 15th December 1990. Brian had been asked to compose the incidental music for 'The Scottish Play', which was to feature Roy Marsden in the lead role.

Brian was nervous about such an undertaking. He'd never stepped quite so far out of his sturdy rock'n'roll boots before. But it was a challenge, and as far as he was concerned, he'd carry it through to the end:

"On one level, I was very confident, on the other I was thinking: 'My God, what if these people don't like what I do?'. But, in fact, when I brought the first piece of music in after living with it for, I guess, two weeks' rehearsals, they all individually came over and said: 'That's great Brian. That's just what we want'. There was an immense sense of relief that I could go forward and do it then and know that I had their backing.

"I had a great time, because I did it very interactively with the players, and I wrote around their interpretation. Some people likened the resulting piece to 'Mars' from the 'Planet Suite', which I thought was quite a compliment really, coz part of it's magical and part of it was meant to be an expression of hopeless war. In the end, I did very little guitar, but towards the close of the play, there's this battle scene, and I just thought 'This is the point where a guitar has to kick in', and so I put it in there, and I just took it to another level. That's the bit I enjoyed most."

Roger, meanwhile, continued to work with The Cross, and the band released their second album, 'Mad, Bad And Dangerous To Know'. In February, Queen were invited to appear at the annual Brit Awards, but pulled out at the last minute. Triggering speculation over Freddie's health again. But he needed his rest, even if it meant stirring up the gossip-mongers. In between recording sessions in Montreux, he would fly back to London, spending time at last in his home in Kensington. Surrounded by loving, protective friends, and his little troupe of cats, Freddie was in good company.

Obviously, the band were spending a great deal of time discussing their future. They wanted to keep everything ticking over as if nothing was wrong, presenting a strong, united face to the world. Changing record companies was hardly a move to prompt rumours of an imminent split and terminating their contracts with EMI and Capitol, Queen signed a new deal with the Disney-owned Hollywood Records in America.

And the awards kept flooding in, the most honourable being from the BPI for their outstanding contribution to British Music, and Queen subsequently held an all-night Twentieth Anniversary party. A little premature perhaps, as their official Twentieth Anniversary wouldn't be until the following year. But maybe they had good reason for such early celebrations.

1991 *was* officially Queen's Twentieth Anniversary. Although the band had started in

1970, John Deacon hadn't completed the band's line-up until February 1971.

In January 1991, Queen released their grandest album for a long, long time. 'Innuendo', Queen's fourteenth studio creation, was almost turning the band full-circle, back where they had come from. It boasted the pomposity of 'A Night At The Opera' and 'A Day At The Races', with its massive harmonies and pristine production. There was almost too much going on within the twelve songs - too much to notice where, perhaps, the innuendoes lay. That would come later.

'Innuendo' sat regally atop the album charts, soon to be joined by the single of the same name. A remarkable, six-and-a-half minutes of grand gestures, a melée of opera, Spanish flamenco and rock. It was 'Bohemian Rhapsody' 1991-style, and, coincidentally, it was the first single to break 'Bo Rap's record five minutes and fifty-five seconds in 1976. The accompanying video similarly broke the 'Bohemian Rhapsody' video's record. The staggering mix of animation and computer trickery won director Jerry Hibbert and The Torpedo Twins the U.S. 'Gold Camera Award'.

Compared to 'Bohemian Rhapsody's paltry £4500 budget and shooting time of four hours, 'Innuendo' cost a staggering £120,000 in technical sophistication, and took eight weeks to produce. Jerry Hibbert:

"I had no brief at all, except for some artwork that had already been done for the album cover. It was very much a blank piece of paper for me. But they did like the stuff I did for the 'South Bank Show', and said they wanted some sort of adult-oriented animation - something unusual. Well, I think that's what they got."

Unfortunately, the video once again prompted rumours of Freddie's ill health. There was no original footage of the band within 'Innuendo' - Jerry Hibbert had had to use existing images of each band member to work with, drawing over and animating each figure in turn. In publicity shots for the album and single, Freddie looked thin and gaunt.

Perhaps that was the reason Freddie insisted on appearing in the flesh in the next video, 'I'm Going Slightly Mad', released with the single on 4th March 1991. The £200,000 shoot, entirely engineered by Freddie himself, was a comical black-and-white pastiche, with the singer featured heavily from beginning to end. But, smothered as he was with pan-stick white make-up, and donning a variety of headgear, including a bunch of bananas (!), the rumours unfortunately did not abate.

Through 'Headlong' on 13th May and the now-emotive 'The Show Must Go On' on 14th October, the band were at their best, their most entertaining, their most prolific. The more the lyrics in 'Innuendo' were studied, the more it became apparent that the days of Queen producing what Freddie would call 'throwaway pop' were over. And still, Queen carried on as normal, allowing not a glimpse of their real feelings to emerge from behind the smiles.

When Freddie's former manager, Paul Prenter, died of Aids in Dublin in the summer, the band were shaken. It was like the hour-hand of a clock moving closer and closer to midnight. But still, 'everything was hunky-dory'. EMI released a Twentieth Anniversary 'Greatest Hits' package in October. Just like its Tenth Anniversary predecessor, the set comprised the 'Greatest Hits II' album, 'Greatest Flix II' video and 'Greatest Pix II' book. Queen didn't want their fans to forget their anniversary. Brian took in a brief 'radio tour' of the States to promote 'Innuendo' and his own solo album, which was scheduled for release in 1992, to follow his single, 'Just One Life'. In November, he appeared with Steve Vai, Joe Satriani, Joe Walsh and others at the Expo '92 'Guitar Legends' festival, a mass gathering of the world's most influential guitarists in Seville, Spain. And, on 18th November, he appeared with major Queen fans Extreme at the first of their two Hammersmith Odeon gigs. On 20th April 1992, Extreme would release a single, 'Song Of Love', with a cover of Queen's 'Love Of My Life' on the B-side, featuring Brian himself.

In the public's eye, Queen were back, stronger than ever, with a blinding album that indicated they'd be around for a long time yet. Even as reports reached the press that clusters of fans were keeping a constant vigil outside Freddie's home, that his mother and father, Jer and Bomi, and close friends such as Mary Austin, Dave Clark, Elton John and the band were paying regular visits to 'Garden Lodge', some people still didn't want to believe the worst. Even when Dr Gizzard, Head of the Aids Unit at London's Westminster Hospital, paid Freddie a visit in November, surely it didn't mean... Not yet. Freddie was fine.

On Sunday 24th November 1991, Freddie Mercury, née Bulsara, died peacefully at his home in Kensington. Close friend Dave Clark was present at the time.

CHAPTER SIXTEEN

IS THIS THE WORLD WE CREATED?

*"Freddie's life definitely changed the world, and I
think his death is already changing it too..."*
(Brian May)

"Following the enormous conjecture in the
press over the last two weeks, I wish to confirm
that I have tested HIV positive and have Aids. I
felt it correct to keep this information private in
order to protect the privacy of those around me.
However, the time has come for my friends and
fans around the world to know the truth, and I
hope that everyone will join with me in the fight
against this terrible disease."

Freddie's final statement to the world, just days
before he died. A desperate plea to 'All God's
People' to rid the world of the Aids epidemic. He
didn't need to ask. His death had been enough to
spur people on to take the damn virus seriously.

But before getting on with the vital business of
spreading Aids awareness to the world,
everybody - friends and fans alike - wanted first to
pay tribute to Freddie Mercury, the most
dedicated entertainer the rock'n'roll world has
ever seen.

Brian May summed up the band's own feelings
on Freddies death. They had all supported him
during these last months: "It is like a rock
dropping on your head. Watching him die, the
over-riding feeling is one of helplessness. My
father died of cancer, so it was a similar feeling

watching that take a hold, the inevitable way in which the virus takes over. It was terrible to see how much pain he was in but he didn't want any sympathy, he wanted to be treated as normal, and we had lots of laughs and silliness right up to the end."

The night after Freddie's death, the BBC broadcast a tribute to the singer, shakily introduced by one of his closest friends, Elton John. The programme was an appropriate, respectful salute, a catalogue of Queen live and in the studio, with excerpts from interviews - from beginning to end.

Tributes and messages poured into the Queen offices from all over the world. Some of the messages from Freddie's more well-known friends and peers read as follows:

"Freddie was one of the elite few who could really set a stadium alight. Along with millions of fans throughout the world, I will miss his exceptional performance and brilliant voice." (Francis Rossi, Status Quo)

"Freddie Mercury was an incredibly innovative singer and frontman for the band. He was a very good friend of mine and it was a privilege to have known him for some of his life. He was very funny, extremely outrageous, very kind and he was a great musician - one of the great frontmen of rock'n'roll bands... Quite simply, he was one of the most important figures in rock'n'roll in the last twenty years. I will miss him - we will all miss him - for his music, his humanity... We will remember that Freddie Mercury was something special." (Elton John introducing the BBC tribute)

"His death is one of the most devastating things I

*have ever heard. He was a fine artiste and a lovely man.
He was one of the most charismatic men I have ever met
and he will be missed by everyone in the rock business.
Let us hope that he is to be remembered more for his
music than for the awful way in which he seems to have
faded from our lives."* (David Essex)

Whilst these tributes reached the ears of the
world thousands of musicians were paying
homage to Freddie and on records. Extreme, of
course, had thier cover version of 'Love of my
Life', and Americans the Lynch Mob boasted 'Tie
Your Mother Down' on thier May - released
album. 'Bohemian Rhapsody' was found
enhancing a particularly memorable scene from
the summer - released movie 'Wayne's World'. It
seemed that everyone wanted to pay thier last
respects to the great Freddie Mercury.

The funeral was a subdued affair. There
was no glitter, no glamour - instead, a
carpet of flowers bathed the crematorium
floor, where a respectful number of people,
Freddie's family, his closest friends, the band,
lined up to pay their last respects to Frederick
Bulsara, the little buck-toothed boy from Zanzibar,
who'd grown into the fabulously outrageous,
internationally-adored Freddie Mercury of Queen.
The press coverage was, for once, respectful. How
ironic.

Now the formalities were over, there was work
to be done. Freddie would not have allowed
anybody to waste time sitting back on their laurels
mourning for him when the Aids epidemic still
raged onwards. He had left Brian, Roger and John
a legacy - and also a method of lifting them from
their grief. They had no time for solo ventures
either, not for the moment anyway. The most

immediate plan was to raise money for the Terence Higgins Trust, the Aids charity to whom Freddie'd left the bulk of his estate.

The band set to work immediately. On 9th December 1991, 'Bohemian Rhapsody' was re-released, as a double A-sided single with 'These Are The Days Of Our Lives' from 'Innuendo'. The videos for the two songs ironically represented Freddie's first and last video.

All proceeds from the single were to go to the Terence Higgins Trust. The single raced to No 1.... But the band had bigger plans than that, as Roger revealed shortly after Freddie's death: "Freddie felt that by making the announcement that he had Aids, he could make something positive out of this awful thing that's happening, and make sure his death meant something. We intend to carry his wishes through. We're thinking next year of doing some kind of event, probably in his name, that will be something positive and will raise a lot of money we hope.

"We never spoke to Freddie about doing this, it was just a quietly accepted thing."

Roger was referring to early plans for 'A Concert For Life', the Freddie Mercury Tribute Concert for Aids Awareness at Wembley Stadium on 20th April 1992 - Easter Monday. At that early stage, no concrete plans had been set, but it would turn out to be a massive, moving tribute to Freddie. The event, broadcast world-wide to an estimated half a billion people in several countries, would include the following major artists who asked specifically to contribute their talents, so that they could personally pay homage to Freddie: Guns N'Roses, Elton John, David Bowie, George

Michael, Roger Daltrey, Def Leppard, Extreme, Ian Hunter, Annie Lennox, Metallica, Robert Plant, Mick Ronson, Seal, Spinal Tap, U2 (via satellite from Sacremento, California), Paul Young, Zucchero - and of course, Brian May, John Deacon and Roger Taylor.

All 72,000 tickets for the concert sold out in a record three hours! Brian was bowled over when he heard the news:

"Freddie has given us such a magnificent platform to make money for the Aids project with no problem at all. We can raise awareness of it, which is definitely happening already. Freddie's death I think helped people to view homosexuality differently, at least I hope so. For us, it's been very difficult to talk about, because it was his business while it was going on. But I think the fact that he was so open about it forced people to stop being coy about talking about it. God knows, it's about time."

Roger:

"AIDS affects us all. We see the Wembley tribute as an international celebration of Freddie's life and the fulfilment of his wish to get this message across."

"Freddie would've loved the idea of all these stars turning up for him. He always liked to do things properly and in a big way."

'A Concert For Life' would be Queen's first appearance at Wembley since 1986. Ironically, a live album of that original performance, 'Queen Live At Wembley' would be released on 25th May 1992.

Freddie probably would not have believed the effect his death has had on people's awareness of Aids. Brian had admitted that he and the rest of the band had never really been able to talk openly about Freddie's bisexuality, and that his death had at least stripped away the 'taboo' sensitivity of bisexuality, homosexuality and Aids for him personally. Now that he's campaigning for the Aids movement, Freddie has in a sense forced him to stop being so coy about the subject, for once in his life! Freddie certainly did not die in vain. And, according to Roger, nor did he die unhappy, although he was in pain. He was in a "stable, loving relationship" when he died and, contrary to press reports, he wasn't "miserable" at all. Freddie, after all, hinted many times that he didn't expect to survive long enough for old age:

"I don't expect to make old bones. What's more, I really don't care. I certainly don't have any aspirations to live to seventy, it would be boring."

And he was certainly aware of the achievements he'd made in his life:

"I have lived a full life, and if I am dead tomorrow, I don't care a damn. I really have done it all."

Indeed. And Freddie really did tie up all the loose ends before passing away too. Throughout 'Innuendo', he says everything he may've forgotten to say before. The two charming songs to his cats, 'Delilah' and 'Bijou' seem to be Freddie's way of saying goodbye to his two beloved friends. 'The Hitman' could be a vicious attack on Aids. And, of course, in that grand opening title-track, he even makes early apology for the mass of innuendoes within the album:

'don't take offence at my innuendo'. But I would feel ashamed of dissecting 'Innuendo' too much - it would be like peering into somebody's bedroom.

You see, whilst it's easy to analyse, there will be a school of thought from those close to Freddie that it's all to easy to surrender to morbid curiosity. How easy to scrutinise the faces of the band in Freddie's last video, for example. 'These Are The Days Of Our Lives' was, of course, poignant - the words could be said to be unbearably sad, but only if placed in the context of Freddie's death (it's hard not to be moved). The faces of the band could appear to be full of sorrow, but only if placed in the context of Freddie's death.

The video and song should be viewed through objective eyes - imagine Freddie's still alive, and you'll discover that 'These Are The Days Of Our Lives' is just a song about retrospect, nostalgic memories of anyone's life, not just Freddie's. But, of course, it doesn't just stop there. I was guilty myself of endlessly studying lyrics from Queen's albums as far back as 1985, when Freddie may've discovered he had Aids. Reading fathoms of knowledge, suggesting reasons for certain lyrics. And then, finally, 'understanding' the motives behind 'I'm Going Slightly Mad' and 'The Show Must Go On'....

As Brian said after Freddie's death: "There're a lot of things in a lot of the songs if you look back now. You'll find a lot of them have some sort of bearing on what was going on in the end. But, of course, our songs were never generally about one thing. There're usually different levels in a lot of our songs."

It's nobody's business but Freddie's. Like any song, his lyrics have different connotations for different people. Perhaps, having scoured those songs for the meaning of Freddie's life during the last eighteen months, we should now get on with relating them to our own lives. The show, after all, must go on.

For Queen, however, it cannot possibly go on. Whatever anyone says, Queen broke up when Freddie died. Knebworth Festival 1986 was their last gig, 'Innuendo' the last album.

Brian with his solo venture, Roger with The Cross, John with whatever - I hope, as we all do, that they will continue with their own projects.

'The Show Must Go On', therefore, would be the most inappropriate quote to end this book on Queen, the band. Instead, I'd like to take a couple of lines out of that song to say an appropriate farewell to Freddie:

> *'My soul is painted like the*
> *wings of butterflies, Fairytales of*
> *yesterday will grow but never die..'*

Indeed.

THE END

Kingsfleet Publications
The Power House, Tandridge Court Farm, Tandridge Lane, Oxted, Surrey RH8 9NJ